Deep Learning AMI Developer Guide

A catalogue record for this book is available from the Hong Kong Public Libraries.

Published in Hong Kong by Samurai Media Limited.

Email: info@samuraimedia.org

ISBN 9789888407705

Contents

What Is the AWS Deep Learning AMI?

Welcome to the User Guide for the AWS Deep Learning AMI.

The AWS Deep Learning AMI (DLAMI) is your one-stop shop for deep learning in the cloud. This customized machine instance is available in most Amazon EC2 regions for a variety of instance types, from a small CPU-only instance to the latest high-powered multi-GPU instances. It comes preconfigured with NVIDIA CUDA and NVIDIA cuDNN, as well as the latest releases of the most popular deep learning frameworks.

About This Guide

This guide will help you launch and use the DLAMI. It covers several use cases that are common for deep learning, for both training and inference. Choosing the right AMI for your purpose and the kind of instances you may prefer is also covered. The DLAMI comes with several tutorials for each of the frameworks. You will find instructions on how to configure Jupyter to run the tutorials in your browser.

Prerequisites

You should be familiar with command line tools and basic Python to successfully run the DLAMI. Tutorials on how to use each framework are provided by the frameworks themselves, however, this guide can show you how to activate each one and find the appropriate tutorials to get started.

Example DLAMI Uses

Learning about deep learning: The DLAMI is a great choice for learning or teaching machine learning and deep learning frameworks. It takes the headache away from troubleshooting the installations of each framework and getting them to play along on the same computer. The DLAMI comes with a Jupyter notebook and makes it easy to run the tutorials provided by the frameworks for people new to machine learning and deep learning.

App development: If you're an app developer and are interested in using deep learning to make your apps utilize the latest advances in AI, the DLAMI is the perfect test bed for you. Each framework comes with tutorials on how to get started with deep learning, and many of them have model zoos that make it easy to try out deep learning without having to create the neural networks yourself or to do any of the model training. Some examples show you how to build an image detection application in just a few minutes, or how to build a speech recognition app for your own chatbot.

Machine learning and data analytics: If you're a data scientist or interested in processing your data with deep learning, you'll find that many of the frameworks have support for R and Spark. You will find tutorials on how to do simple regressions, all the way up to building scalable data processing systems for personalization and predictions systems.

Research: If you're a researcher and want to try out a new framework, test out a new model, or train new models, the DLAMI and AWS capabilities for scale can alleviate the pain of tedious installations and management of multiple training nodes. You can use EMR and AWS CloudFormation templates to easily launch a full cluster of instances that are ready to go for scalable training.

Note

While your initial choice might be to upgrade your instance type up to a larger instance with more GPUs (up to 8), you can also scale horizontally by creating a cluster of DLAMI instances. To quickly set up a cluster, you can use the predefined AWS CloudFormation template. Check out Resources and Support for more information on cluster builds.

Features of the DLAMI

Preinstalled Frameworks

There are currently three primary flavors of the DLAMI with other variations related to the operating system (OS) and software versions:

- Deep Learning AMI with Conda - frameworks installed separately using `conda` packages and separate Python environments
- Deep Learning AMI with Source Code - frameworks installed from source together in the same Python environment
- Deep Learning Base AMI - no frameworks installed; only NVIDIA CUDA and other dependencies

The new Deep Learning AMI with Conda uses Anaconda environments to isolate each framework, so you can switch between them at will and not worry about their dependencies conflicting. The Deep Learning AMI with Source Code has all of the deep learning frameworks installed into the same Python environment, along with the frameworks' source.

For more information on selecting the best DLAMI for you, take a look at Getting Started.

This is the full list supported frameworks between Deep Learning AMI with Conda and Deep Learning AMI with Source Code:

- Apache MXNet
- Caffe
- Caffe2
- CNTK
- Keras
- PyTorch
- TensorFlow
- Theano**
- Torch*

Note
* Only available on the Deep Learning AMI with Source Code.
** Theano is being phased out, as it is no longer an active project.

Preinstalled GPU Software

Even if you use a CPU-only instance, the DLAMI will have NVIDIA CUDA and NVIDIA cuDNN. The installed software is the same regardless of the instance type. Keep in mind that GPU-specific tools only work on an instance that has at least one GPU. More information on this is covered in the Selecting the Instance Type for DLAMI.

- NVIDIA CUDA 9
- NVIDIA cuDNN 7
- CUDA 8 is available as well. See the CUDA Installations and Framework Bindings for more information.

Model Serving and Visualization

Deep Learning AMI with Conda comes preinstalled with two kinds of model servers, one for MXNet and one for TensorFlow, as well as TensorBoard, for model visualizations.

- Running Model Server for Apache MXNet on the Deep Learning AMI with Conda
- TensorFlow Serving
- TensorBoard

Getting Started

How to Get Started with the DLAMI

Getting started is easy. Included in this guide are tips on picking the DLAMI that's right for you, selecting an instance type that fits your use case and budget, and Resources and Support that describe custom setups that may be of interest. Or you can go straight to the latest DLAMI on the AWS Marketplace, Deep Learning AMI with Conda, and spin up an instance from there.

If you're new to using AWS or using Amazon EC2, start with the Deep Learning AMI with Conda. If you're familiar with Amazon EC2 and other AWS services like Amazon EMR, Amazon EFS, or Amazon S3, and are interested in integrating those services for projects that need distributed training or inference, then check out Resources and Support to see if one fits your use case.

If you're already familiar with using AMIs and want to spin one up now, you can go to the AMI Marketplace now. But first we recommend that you check out Choosing Your DLAMI to get an idea of which instance type might be best for your application.

Another option is this quick tutorial: Launch a AWS Deep Learning AMI (in 10 minutes).

Next Step
Choosing Your DLAMI

Choosing Your DLAMI

If you run a search for deep learning in the AMI Marketplace, you may find there are many options, and it's not clear which is best suited for your use case. This section helps you decide. When we refer to a DLAMI, often this is really a group of AMIs centered around a common type or functionality. There are three variables that define these types and/or functionality:

- Conda versus Source versus Base

- CUDA 8 versus CUDA 9

- Amazon Linux versus Ubuntu versus Windows

The rest of the topics in this guide will help further inform you and go into more details.

- Deep Learning AMI with Conda
- Deep Learning Base AMI
- Deep Learning AMI with Source Code
- CUDA Installations and Framework Bindings
- DLAMI Operating System Options

Next Up
Deep Learning AMI with Conda

Deep Learning AMI with Conda

Use the Launching and Configuring a DLAMI guide to continue with one of these DLAMI.

- Deep Learning AMI (Ubuntu)
- Deep Learning AMI (Amazon Linux)

These DLAMIs are available in these regions:

Region	Code
US East (Ohio)	ec2-us-east-2
US East (N. Virginia)	ec2-us-east-1
US West (N. California)	ec2-us-west-1
US West (Oregon)	ec2-us-west-2
Beijing (China)	cn-north-1
Asia Pacific (Mumbai)	ec2-ap-south-1
Asia Pacific (Seoul)	ec2-ap-northeast-2
Asia Pacific (Singapore)	ec2-ap-southeast-1
Asia Pacific (Sydney)	ec2-ap-southeast-2
Asia Pacific (Tokyo)	ec2-ap-northeast-1
Canada (Central)	ec2-ca-central-1
EU (Frankfurt)	ec2-eu-central-1
EU (Ireland)	ec2-eu-west-1
EU (London)	ec2-eu-west-2
EU (Paris)	ec2-eu-west-3
SA (Sao Paulo)	ec2-sa-east-1

Deep Learning Base AMI

Use the Launching and Configuring a DLAMI guide to continue with one of these DLAMI.

- Deep Learning Base AMI (Ubuntu)
- Deep Learning Base AMI (Amazon Linux)

These DLAMIs are available in these regions:

Region	Code
US East (Ohio)	ec2-us-east-2
US East (N. Virginia)	ec2-us-east-1
US West (N. California)	ec2-us-west-1
US West (Oregon)	ec2-us-west-2
Beijing (China)	cn-north-1
Asia Pacific (Mumbai)	ec2-ap-south-1
Asia Pacific (Seoul)	ec2-ap-northeast-2
Asia Pacific (Singapore)	ec2-ap-southeast-1
Asia Pacific (Sydney)	ec2-ap-southeast-2
Asia Pacific (Tokyo)	ec2-ap-northeast-1
Canada (Central)	ec2-ca-central-1
EU (Frankfurt)	ec2-eu-central-1
EU (Ireland)	ec2-eu-west-1
EU (London)	ec2-eu-west-2
EU (Paris)	ec2-eu-west-3
SA (Sao Paulo)	ec2-sa-east-1

Deep Learning AMI with Source Code

Important
These DLAMI are no longer being updated. It is advised to use the Deep Learning AMI with Conda or Deep Learning Base AMI.

Use the Launching and Configuring a DLAMI guide to continue with one of these DLAMI.

- Deep Learning AMI with Source Code (CUDA 9, Ubuntu)

- Deep Learning AMI with Source Code (CUDA 9, Amazon Linux)

- Deep Learning AMI with Source Code (CUDA 8, Ubuntu)

- Deep Learning AMI with Source Code (CUDA 8, Amazon Linux)

These DLAMIs are available in these regions:

Region	Code
US East (Ohio)	ec2-us-east-2
US East (N. Virginia)	ec2-us-east-1
US West (N. California)	ec2-us-west-1
US West (Oregon)	ec2-us-west-2
Beijing (China)	cn-north-1
Asia Pacific (Mumbai)	ec2-ap-south-1
Asia Pacific (Seoul)	ec2-ap-northeast-2
Asia Pacific (Singapore)	ec2-ap-southeast-1
Asia Pacific (Sydney)	ec2-ap-southeast-2
Asia Pacific (Tokyo)	ec2-ap-northeast-1
Canada (Central)	ec2-ca-central-1
EU (Frankfurt)	ec2-eu-central-1
EU (Ireland)	ec2-eu-west-1
EU (London)	ec2-eu-west-2
EU (Paris)	ec2-eu-west-3
SA (Sao Paulo)	ec2-sa-east-1

CUDA Installations and Framework Bindings

Deep learning is all pretty cutting edge, however, each framework offers "stable" versions. These stable versions may not work with the latest CUDA or cuDNN implementation and features. How do you decide? This ultimately points to your use case and the features you require. If you are not sure, then go with the latest Deep Learning AMI with Conda. It has official pip binaries of all frameworks with both CUDA 8 and CUDA 9, using whichever most recent version is supported by each framework.

Look at our guide on Stable versus Bleeding Edge for further guidance.

CUDA Support
The Deep Learning AMI with Source Code's CUDA version and the frameworks supported for each:

- Deep Learning AMI with CUDA 9: Apache MXNet, Caffe2, PyTorch, TensorFlow

- Deep Learning AMI with CUDA 8: Apache MXNet, Caffe, Caffe2, CNTK, PyTorch, Theano, TensorFlow, and Torch

Specific framework version numbers can be found in the DLAMI: Release Notes

Choose this DLAMI type or learn more about the different DLAMIs with the Next Up option.

Choose one of the CUDA versions and review the full list of DLAMIs that have that version in the Appendix, or learn more about the different DLAMIs with the Next Up option.

- Deep Learning AMI with CUDA 9

- Deep Learning AMI with CUDA 8

Next Up
DLAMI Operating System Options

DLAMI Operating System Options

DLAMIs are offered in the operating systems listed below. If you're more familiar with CentOS or RedHat, you will be more comfortable with AWS Deep Learning AMI, Amazon Linux Versions. Otherwise, you may find the AWS Deep Learning AMI, Ubuntu Versions more to your liking.

If you need Windows as your OS, then you have a couple options found here: AWS Deep Learning AMI, Windows Versions.

Choose one of the operating systems and review their full list in the Appendix, or go on to the next steps for picking your AMI and instance type.

- AWS Deep Learning AMI, Amazon Linux Versions
- AWS Deep Learning AMI, Ubuntu Versions
- AWS Deep Learning AMI, Windows Versions

As mentioned in the Getting Started overview, you have a few options for accessing a DLAMI, but first you should assess what instance type you need. You should also identify the region that you're going to use.

Next Up
Selecting the Instance Type for DLAMI

Selecting the Instance Type for DLAMI

Selecting the instance type can be another challenge, but we'll make this easier for you with a few pointers on how to choose the best one. Remember, the DLAMI is free, but the underlying compute resources are not.

- If you're new to deep learning, then you probably want an "entry-level" instance with a single GPU.

- If you're budget conscious, then you will need to start a bit smaller and look at the CPU-only instances.

- If you're interested in running a trained model for inference and predictions (and not training), then you might want a CPU instance with a lot of memory, or even a cluster of these for high-volume services.

- If you're interested in training a model with a lot of data, then you might want a larger instance or even a cluster of GPU instances.

DLAMIs are not available in every region, but it is possible to copy DLAMIs to the region of your choice. See Copying an AMI for more info. Each region supports a different range of instance types and often an instance type has a slightly different cost in different regions. On each DLAMI main page, you will see a list of instance costs. Note the region selection list and be sure you pick a region that's close to you or your customers. If you plan to use more than one DLAMI and potentially create a cluster, be sure to use the same region for all of nodes in the cluster.

- For more detail on instances, check out EC2 Instance Types.

- For a more info on regions, visit EC2 Regions.

So with all of those points in mind, make note of the instance type that best applies to your use case and budget. The rest of the topics in this guide help further inform you and go into more detail.

Important
The Deep Learning AMIs include drivers, software, or toolkits developed, owned, or provided by NVIDIA Corporation. You agree to use these NVIDIA drivers, software, or toolkits only on Amazon EC2 instances that include NVIDIA hardware.

- Recommended GPU Instances
- Recommended CPU Instances
- Pricing for the DLAMI

Next Up
Recommended GPU Instances

Recommended GPU Instances

A GPU instance is recommended for most deep learning purposes. Training new models will be faster on a GPU instance than a CPU instance. You can scale sub-linearly when you have multi-GPU instances or if you use distributed training across many instances with GPUs.

- Amazon EC2 P3 Instances have up to 8 NVIDIA Tesla V100 GPUs.

- Amazon EC2 P2 Instances have up to 16 NVIDIA NVIDIA K80 GPUs.

- Amazon EC2 G3 Instances have up to 4 NVIDIA Tesla M60 GPUs.

- Check out EC2 Instance Types and choose Accelerated Computing to see the different GPU instance options.

Next Up
Recommended CPU Instances

Recommended CPU Instances

Whether you're on a budget, learning about deep learning, or just want to run a prediction service, you have many affordable options in the CPU category. Some frameworks take advantage of Intel's MKL DNN, which will speed up training and inference on C5 (not available in all regions), C4, and C3 CPU instance types.

- Amazon EC2 C5 Instances have up to 72 Intel vCPUs.
- Amazon EC2 C4 Instances have up to 36 Intel vCPUs.
- Check out EC2 Instance Types and look for **Compute Optimized** to see the different CPU instance options.

Note
C5 instances (not available in all regions) excel at scientific modelling, batch processing, distributed analytics, high-performance computing (HPC), and machine/deep learning inference.

Important
If you plan to use Caffe, you should choose a GPU instance instead. On the DLAMI, Caffe only works with with GPU support, and cannot be run in CPU mode.

Next Up
Pricing for the DLAMI

Pricing for the DLAMI

The DLAMI is free, however, you are still responsible for Amazon EC2 or other AWS service costs. The included deep learning frameworks are free, and each has its own open source licenses. The GPU software from NVIDIA is free, and has its own licenses as well.

How is it free, but not free? What are the "Amazon EC2 or other AWS service costs"?

This is a common question. Some instance types on Amazon EC2 are labeled as free. These are typically the smaller instances, and it is possible to run the DLAMI on one of these free instances. This means that it is entirely free when you only use that instance's capacity. If you decide that you want a more powerful instance, with more CPU cores, more disk space, more RAM, and one or more GPUs, then these are most likely not in the free-tier instance class. This means that you will need to pay for those costs. One way to think of it is that the software is still free, but you have to pay for the underlying hardware that you're using.

Take a look at Selecting the Instance Type for DLAMI for more information on what size of instance to choose and what kinds of things you can expect from each type.

Next Step
Launching and Configuring a DLAMI

Launching and Configuring a DLAMI

If you're here you should already have a good idea of which AMI you want to launch. If not, choose a DLAMI using the AMI selection guidelines found throughout Getting Started or use the full listing of AMIs in the Appendix section, AMI Options.

You should also know which instance type and region you're going to choose. If not, browse Selecting the Instance Type for DLAMI.

Note
We will use p2.xlarge as the default instance type in the examples. Just replace this with whichever instance type you have in mind.

- Step 1: Launch a DLAMI
- EC2 Console
- Marketplace Search
- Step 2: Connect to the DLAMI
- Step 3: Secure Your DLAMI Instance
- Step 4: Test Your DLAMI
- Clean Up
- Set up a Jupyter Notebook Server

Step 1: Launch a DLAMI

Note

For this walkthrough, we might make references specific to the Deep Learning AMI (Ubuntu). Even if you select a different DLAMI, you should be able to follow this guide.

Launch the instance

1. You have a couple routes for launching DLAMI. Choose one:

   - EC2 Console

   - Marketplace Search **Tip**
     *CLI Option: *If you choose to spin up a DLAMI using the AWS CLI, you will need the AMI's ID, the region and instance type, and your security token information. Be sure you have your AMI and instance IDs ready. If you haven't set up the AWS CLI yet, do that first using the guide for Installing the AWS Command Line Interface.

2. After you have completed the steps of one of those options, wait for the instance to be ready. This usually takes only a few minutes. You can verify the status of the instance in the EC2 Console.

EC2 Console

1. Open the EC2 Console.

2. Note your current region in the top-most navigation. If this isn't your desired AWS Region, change this option before proceeding. For more information, see EC2 Regions.

3. Choose **Launch Instance**.

4. Search for the desired instance by name:

    1. Choose **AWS Marketplace**, or...

    2. Choose **QuickStart**. Only a subset of available DLAMI will be listed here.

    3. Search for `AWS Deep Learning AMI`. Also look for the subtype, such as your desired OS, and if you want Base, Conda, Source, etc.

    4. Browse the options, and then click **Select** on your choice.

5. Review the details, and then choose **Continue**.

6. Choose an instance type.

7. Choose **Review and Launch**.

8. Review the details and pricing. Choose **Launch**.

Tip
Check out for a walk-through with screenshots!

Next Step
Step 2: Connect to the DLAMI

Marketplace Search

1. Browse the AWS Marketplace and search for AWS Deep Learning AMI.

2. Browse the options, and then click **Select** on your choice.

3. Review the details, and then choose **Continue**.

4. Review the details and make note of the **Region**. If this isn't your desired AWS Region, change this option before proceeding. For more information, see EC2 Regions.

5. Choose an instance type.

6. Choose a key pair, use your default one, or create a new one.

7. Review the details and pricing.

8. Choose **Launch with 1-Click**.

Next Step
Step 2: Connect to the DLAMI

Step 2: Connect to the DLAMI

Connect to the DLAMI that you launched from a client (Windows, MacOS, or Linux). For more information, see Connect to Your Linux Instance in the *Amazon EC2 User Guide for Linux Instances*.

Keep a copy of the SSH login command handy if you want to do the Jupyter setup after logging in. You will use a variation of it to connect to the Jupyter webpage.

Tip
If you launch an Amazon Linux instance, the connect dialog box has "root@" in the SSH login command. This should be replaced with "ec2-user@".

Next Step
Step 4: Test Your DLAMI

Step 3: Secure Your DLAMI Instance

Always keep your operating system and other installed software up to date by applying patches and updates as soon as they become available.

If you are using Amazon Linux or Ubuntu, when you login to your DLAMI, you are notified if updates are available and see instructions for updating. For further information on Amazon Linux maintenance, see Updating Instance Software. For Ubuntu instances, refer to the official Ubuntu documentation.

On Windows, check Windows Update regularly for software and security updates. If you prefer, have updates applied automatically.

Important

For information about the Meltdown and Spectre vulnerabilities and how to patch your operating system to address them, see Security Bulletin AWS-2018-013.

Step 4: Test Your DLAMI

Depending on your DLAMI version, you have different testing options:

- Deep Learning AMI with Conda – go to Using the Deep Learning AMI with Conda.

- Deep Learning AMI with Source Code – refer to your desired framework's getting started documentation.

- Deep Learning Base AMI – refer to your desired framework's installation documentation.

You can also create a Jupyter notebook, try out tutorials, or start coding in Python. For more information, see Set up a Jupyter Notebook Server.

Clean Up

When you no longer need the DLAMI, you can stop it or terminate it to avoid incurring continuing charges. Stopping an instance will keep it around so you can resume it later. Your configurations, files, and other non-volatile information is being stored in a volume on Amazon S3. You will be charged the small S3 fee to retain the volume while the instance is stopped, but you will no longer be charged for the compute resources while it is in the stopped state. When your start the instance again, it will mount that volume and your data will be there. If you terminate an instance, it is gone, and you cannot start it again. Your data actually still resides on S3, so to prevent any further charges you need to delete the volume as well. For more instructions, see Terminate Your Instance in the *Amazon EC2 User Guide for Linux Instances.*

Set up a Jupyter Notebook Server

Jupyter Notebook is a web application that allows you to manage notebook documents using a web browser.

To set up a Jupyter notebook, you:

- Configure the Jupyter notebook server on your Amazon EC2 instance.
- Configure your client so that you can connect to the Jupyter notebook server. We provide configuration instructions for Windows, macOS, and Linux clients.
- Test the setup by logging in to the Jupyter notebook server.

For more information about Jupyter notebooks, see Jupyter.

- Configure Jupyter Notebook on Your DLAMI
- Custom SSL and Server Configuration
- Start the Jupyter notebook server
- Configure the Client to Connect to the Jupyter Server
- Test by Logging in to the Jupyter notebook server

Configure Jupyter Notebook on Your DLAMI

To use Jupyter, you need to open port 8888 (or one of your choosing) on your instance's firewall. You also can set up an SSL certificate and default password, but this is optional. Once the port is open you'll launch the server, then you'll SSH to your server and create a tunnel for you to access Jupyter's web interface. The following steps walk you through this process.

Open your EC2 dashboard and choose **Security Groups** on the EC2 navigation bar in the **Network & Security** section. On this page, there will be one or more security groups in the list. Find the most recent one (the description has a timestamp in it), select it, choose the **Inbound** tab, and then click **Edit**. Then click **Add Rule**. This adds a new row. Fill in the fields with the following information:

Type : Custom **TCP Rule**

Protocol: TCP

Port Range: 8888

Source: Anywhere (0.0.0.0/0,::/0)

Tip
To make Jupyter run a little more seamlessly, you can modify the Jupyter configuration file. In the configuration file, you set some of the values to use for web authentication, including the SSL certificate file path, and a password. You can go through Custom SSL and Server Configuration now or at a later time.

Next Step
Start the Jupyter notebook server

Custom SSL and Server Configuration

Here we set up a Jupyter notebook with SSL and a config file.

Connect to the Amazon EC2 instance, and then complete the following procedure.

Configure the Jupyter server

1. Create an SSL certificate.

```
1 $ cd
2 $ mkdir ssl
3 $ cd ssl
4 $ sudo openssl req -x509 -nodes -days 365 -newkey rsa:1024 -keyout "cert.key" -out "cert.
    pem" -batch
```

2. Create a password. You use this password to log in to the Jupyter notebook server from your client so you can access notebooks on the server.

    1. Open the iPython terminal.

    ```
    1 $ ipython
    ```

    At the iPython prompt, run the `passwd()`command to set the password.

    ```
    1 iPythonPrompt> from IPython.lib import passwd
    2 iPythonPrompt> passwd()
    ```

    You get the password hash (For example, `sha1:examplefc216:3a35a98ed...`).

    2. Record the password hash.

    3. Exit the iPython terminal.

    ```
    1 $ exit
    ```

3. Edit the Jupyter configuration file.

    Find `jupyter_notebook_config.py` in the `~/.jupyter` directory.

4. Update the configuration file to store your password and SSL certificate information.

    1. Open the .config file.

    ```
    1 $ vi ~/.jupyter/jupyter_notebook_config.py
    ```

    2. Paste the following text at the end of the file. You will need to provide your password hash.

    ```
    1 c = get_config()  # Get the config object.
    2 c.NotebookApp.certfile = u'/home/ubuntu/ssl/cert.pem' # path to the certificate we
        generated
    3 c.NotebookApp.keyfile = u'/home/ubuntu/ssl/cert.key' # path to the certificate key we
        generated
    4 c.IPKernelApp.pylab = 'inline'  # in-line figure when using Matplotlib
    5 c.NotebookApp.ip = '*'  # Serve notebooks locally.
    6 c.NotebookApp.open_browser = False  # Do not open a browser window by default when
        using notebooks.
    7 c.NotebookApp.password = 'sha1:fc216:3a35a98ed980b9...'
    ```

Note
If you're using a DLAMI that doesn't have a default Jupyter config file for you, you need to create one.

```
1    ```
2    $ jupyter notebook --generate-config
3    ```
```

Once created, follow the same steps for updating the config with your SSL info.

```
1    This completes Jupyter server configuration\.
```

Next Step
Start the Jupyter notebook server

Start the Jupyter notebook server

Now you can fire up the server by logging in to the instance and running the following commands.

```
1 $ source activate python3
2 $ jupyter notebook
```

If you opened a port different from 8888, update the port parameter to the port you opened. With the server started, you can now connect to it via an SSH tunnel from your client computer. When the server runs, you will see some output from Jupyter confirming that the server is running. At this point, ignore the callout that you can access the server via a localhost URL, because that won't work on a cloud instance.

Note
The reason you need to activate a Python 3 environment is that Jupyter's interface is expecting Python 3 and does not fully support Python 2. Don't worry if you want to use a framework with Python 2. Jupyter will handle that for you when you switch frameworks using the Jupyter web interface. More info on this can be found in Switching Environments with Jupyter.

Next Step
Configure the Client to Connect to the Jupyter Server

Configure the Client to Connect to the Jupyter Server

After configuring your client to connect to the Jupyter notebook server, you can create and access notebooks on the server in your workspace and run your deep learning code on the server.

For configuration information, choose one of the following links.

- Configure a Windows Client
- Configure a Linux Client
- Configure a MacOS Client

Configure a Windows Client

Prepare

Be sure you have the following information, which you need to set up the SSH tunnel:

- The public DNS name of your Amazon EC2 instance. You can find the public DNS name in the EC2 console.

- The key pair for the private key file. For more information about accessing your key pair, see Amazon EC2 Key Pairs in the *Amazon EC2 User Guide for Linux Instances*.

Set up PuTTY

The following step-by-step instructions explain how to connect to your EC2 instance and set up an SSH tunnel using PuTTY, a free SSH client for Windows. If you receive an error while attempting to connect to your instance, see Troubleshooting Connecting to Your Instance. As a prerequisite, download and install PuTTY from the PuTTY download page. If you already have an older version of PuTTY installed, we recommend that you download the latest version. Be sure to install the entire suite.

1. For connecting to your EC2 instance using PuTTY, you first need to convert your private key file (.pem) generated by Amazon EC2 to a format that is recognized by PuTTY (.ppk). You can find the instructions for creating the .ppk file at Connecting to Your Linux Instance from Windows Using PuTTY. Search for "Converting Your Private Key Using PuTTYgen" in that topic.

2. Now open PuTTY and navigate to **Session** under **Category** in the left pane. Enter the following information:

   Connection type: SSH

   Host Name: ubuntu@*YourInstancePublicDNS*

   Port: 22

   Be sure to specify the appropriate user name for your AMI. For example:

   - For an Amazon Linux AMI, the user name is ec2-user.

   - For a RHEL AMI, the user name is ec2-user or root.

   - For an Ubuntu AMI, the user name is ubuntu or root.

   - For a Centos AMI, the user name is centos.

   - For a Fedora AMI, the user name is ec2-user.

   - For SUSE, the user name is ec2-user or root.

   Otherwise, if ec2-user and root don't work, check with the AMI provider.

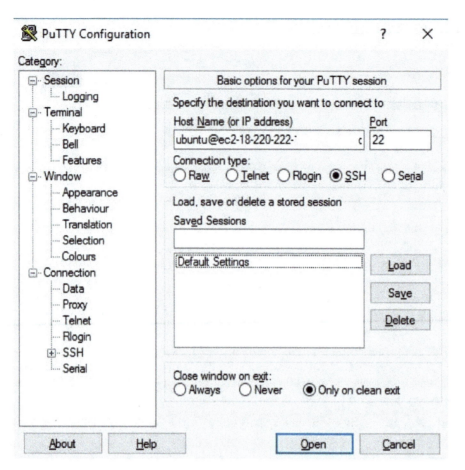

3. Now expand Connection on left pane. Navigate to Auth under SSH. Browse and add the .ppk file you created in Step 1 before. Then click Open at the bottom of the screen.

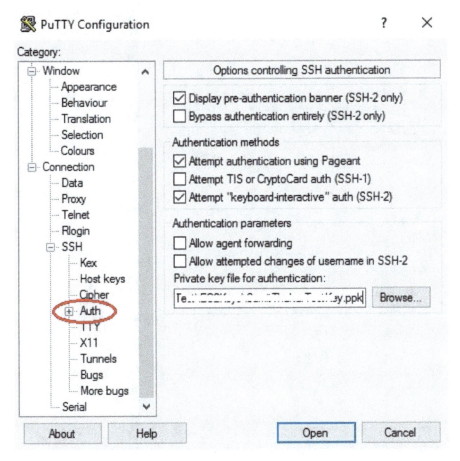

4. If this is the first time you have connected to this instance, PuTTY displays a security alert dialog box that asks whether you trust the host you are connecting to. Choose Yes. A window opens and you are connected to your instance.

5. Now to set up the SSH tunnel to your EC2 instance, right click on the top left corner of your instance's window as highlighted below. It will open a dropdown menu. Select Change Settings from the menu to bring up PuTTY Reconfiguration screen.

6. Navigate to Tunnels under SSH on the left pane. Fill up the Source port and Destination as shown below. Select Local and Auto as port forwarding options. Finally, click Add followed by Apply to finish setting up the SSH tunnel.

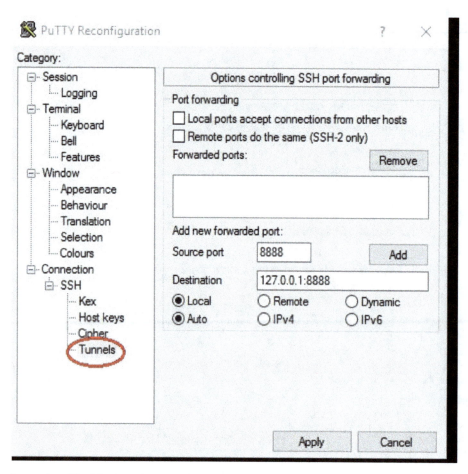

The above simplified instructions give you a quick and easy way to connect to your EC2 instance using PuTTY. If you want to learn more about the topic, you can look at our Connect to Your Linux instance from Windows guide.

Next Step

Test by Logging in to the Jupyter notebook server

Configure a Linux Client

1. Open a terminal.

2. Run the following command to forward all requests on local port 8157 to port 8888 on your remote Amazon EC2 instance. Update the command by replacing *ec2-###-##-##-###.compute-1.amazonaws.com* with the public DNS name of your EC2 instance.

```
1 $ ssh -i ~/mykeypair.pem -L 8157:127.0.0.1:8888 ubuntu@ec2-###-##-##-###.compute-1.
    amazonaws.com
```

This command opens a tunnel between your client and the remote EC2 instance that is running the Jupyter notebook server. After running the command, you can access the Jupyter notebook server at **https://127/.0/.0/.1:8157**/.

Next Step
Test by Logging in to the Jupyter notebook server

Configure a MacOS Client

1. Open a terminal.

2. Run the following command to forward all requests on local port 8157 to port 8888 on your remote Amazon EC2 instance. Update the command by replacing *ec2-###-##-##-###.compute-1.amazonaws.com* with the public DNS name of your EC2 instance, or just use the public IP address.

```
1 $ ssh -i ~/mykeypair.pem -L 8157:127.0.0.1:8888 ubuntu@ec2-###-##-##-###.compute-1.
    amazonaws.com
```

This command opens a tunnel between your client and the remote EC2 instance that is running the Jupyter notebook server. After running the command, you can access the Jupyter notebook server at **http://127/.0/.0/.1:8157**/.

Next Step
Test by Logging in to the Jupyter notebook server

Test by Logging in to the Jupyter notebook server

Now you are ready to log in to the Jupyter notebook server.

Your next step is to test the connection to the server through your browser.

1. In the address bar of your browser, type the following URL.

   - For macOS and Linux clients, type the following URL.

   ```
   1 http://127.0.0.1:8157
   ```

   - For Windows clients, use localhost or the public DNS name of the Amazon EC2 instance and the Jupyter port number. The Jupyter port is typically 8888.

   ```
   1 http://127.0.0.1:8888
   ```

Note
`https` works only if you went through the extra step of Custom SSL and Server Configuration. These examples use `http` instead, but once your SSL cert is configured, you can switch to `https`.

1. If the connection is successful, you see the Jupyter notebook server webpage. At this point, you maybe asked for a password or token. If you did a simple setup without configuring Jupyter, the token is displayed in the terminal window where you launched the server. Look for something like:

   Copy/paste this URL into your browser when you connect for the
   first time, to login with a token: http://localhost:8888/?token=0
   d3f35c9e404882eaaca6e15efdccbcd9a977fee4a8bc083

   Copy the token (the long series of digits), in this case it would be 0
   d3f35c9e404882eaaca6e15efdccbcd9a977fee4a8bc083, and use that to access your Jupyter notebook
   server.

   If, on the other hand, you edited the Jupyter config with a Custom SSL and Server Configuration, type
   the password that you created when you configured the Jupyter notebook server.

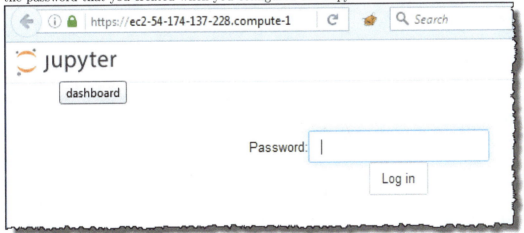

Note

The Jupyter login screen will ask for a token by default. However, if you set up a password, the prompt
will ask for a password instead.

Now you have access to the Jupyter notebook server that is running on the DLAMI. You can create new
notebooks or run the provided Tutorials and Examples.

Tutorials and Examples

- Using the Deep Learning AMI with Conda
- Using the Deep Learning Base AMI
- Running Jupyter Notebook Tutorials
- Apache MXNet
- Caffe2
- Chainer
- CNTK
- Keras
- PyTorch
- TensorFlow
- Theano
- Running Model Server for Apache MXNet on the Deep Learning AMI with Conda
- TensorFlow Serving
- TensorBoard
- 10 Minute Tutorials

The following sections describe how the Deep Learning AMI with Conda can be used to switch environments, run sample code from each of the frameworks, and how to run Jupyter so you can try out different notebook tutorials.

Next Up: Quickstart on switching between frameworks with conda
Using the Deep Learning AMI with Conda

Using the Deep Learning AMI with Conda

- Introduction to the Deep Learning AMI with Conda
- Step 1: Log in to Your DLAMI
- Step 2: Start the MXNet Python 3 Environment
- Step 3: Test Some MXNet Code
- Step 4: Switch to the TensorFlow Environment

Introduction to the Deep Learning AMI with Conda

Conda is an open source package management system and environment management system that runs on Windows, macOS, and Linux. Conda quickly installs, runs, and updates packages and their dependencies. Conda easily creates, saves, loads and switches between environments on your local computer.

The Deep Learning AMI with Conda has been configured for you to easily switch between deep learning environments. The following instructions guide you on some basic commands with conda. They also help you verify that the basic import of the framework is functioning, and that you can run a couple simple operations with the framework. You can then move on to more thorough tutorials provided with the DLAMI or the frameworks' examples found on each frameworks' project site.

Step 1: Log in to Your DLAMI

After you log in to your server, you will see a server "message of the day" (MOTD) describing various conda commands that you can use to switch between the different deep learning frameworks.

```
1  ===============================================================================
2         __|  __|_  )
3         _|  (     /   Deep Learning AMI   (Ubuntu)
4        ___|\___|___|
5  ===============================================================================
6
7  Welcome to Ubuntu 16.04.3 LTS (GNU/Linux 4.4.0-1039-aws x86_64v)
8
9  Please use one of the following commands to start the required environment with the framework of
        your choice:
10 for MXNet(+Keras1) with Python3 (CUDA 9) _____ source activate mxnet_p36
11 for MXNet(+Keras1) with Python2 (CUDA 9) _____ source activate mxnet_p27
12 for TensorFlow(+Keras2) with Python3 (CUDA 8) _____ source activate tensorflow_p36
13 for TensorFlow(+Keras2) with Python2 (CUDA 8) _____ source activate tensorflow_p27
14 for Theano(+Keras2) with Python3 (CUDA 9) _____ source activate theano_p36
15 for Theano(+Keras2) with Python2 (CUDA 9) _____ source activate theano_p27
16 for PyTorch with Python3 (CUDA 8) _____ source activate pytorch_p36
17 for PyTorch with Python2 (CUDA 8) _____ source activate pytorch_p27
18 for CNTK(+Keras2) with Python3 (CUDA 8) _____ source activate cntk_p36
19 for CNTK(+Keras2) with Python2 (CUDA 8) _____ source activate cntk_p27
20 for Caffe2 with Python2 (CUDA 9) _____ source activate caffe2_p27
21 for base Python2 (CUDA 9) _____ source activate python2
22 for base Python3 (CUDA 9) _____ source activate python3
```

Each conda command has the following pattern:

```
source activate framework_python-version
```

For example, you may see `for MXNet(+Keras1)with Python3 (CUDA 9)`_____ `source activate mxnet_p36`, which signifies that the environment has MXNet, Keras 1, Python 3, and CUDA 9. And to activate this environment, the command you would use is:

```
1 $ source activate mxnet_p36
```

The other variation of this would be:

```
1 $ source activate mxnet_p27
```

This signifies that the environment will have MXNet and Python 2 (with Keras 1 and CUDA 9).

Step 2: Start the MXNet Python 3 Environment

We will test MXNet first to give you a general idea of how easy it is.

Note

When you launch your first Conda environment, please be patient while it loads. The Deep Learning AMI with Conda automatically installs the most optimized version of the framework for your EC2 instance upon the framework's first activation. You should not expect subsequent delays.

- Activate the MXNet virtual environment for Python 3.

```
1 $ source activate mxnet_p36
```

This activates the environment for MXNet with Python 3. Alternatively, you could have activated mxnet_p27 to get an environment with Python 2.

Step 3: Test Some MXNet Code

To test your installation, use Python to write MXNet code that creates and prints an array using the `NDArray` API. For more information, see NDArray API.

1. Start the iPython terminal.

```
1 (mxnet_p36)$ ipython
```

2. Import MXNet.

```
1 import mxnet as mx
```

You might see a warning message about a third-party package. You can ignore it.

3. Create a 5x5 matrix, an instance of the `NDArray`, with elements initialized to 0. Print the array.

```
1 mx.ndarray.zeros((5,5)).asnumpy()
```

Verify the result.

```
1 array([[ 0.,   0.,   0.,   0.,   0.],
2        [ 0.,   0.,   0.,   0.,   0.],
3        [ 0.,   0.,   0.,   0.,   0.],
4        [ 0.,   0.,   0.,   0.,   0.],
5        [ 0.,   0.,   0.,   0.,   0.]], dtype=float32)
```

You can find more examples of MXNet in the MXNet tutorials section.

Step 4: Switch to the TensorFlow Environment

Now we will switch to TensorFlow! If you're still in the iPython console use `quit()`, then get ready to switch environments.

1. Activate the TensorFlow virtual environment for Python 3,

```
1 $ source activate tensorflow_p36
```

2. Start the iPython terminal.

```
1 (tensorflow_36)$ ipython
```

3. Run a quick TensorFlow program.

```
1 import tensorflow as tf
2 hello = tf.constant('Hello, TensorFlow!')
3 sess = tf.Session()
4 print(sess.run(hello))
```

You should see "Hello, Tensorflow!" Now you have tested two different deep learning frameworks, and you've seen how to switch between frameworks.

Tip
Refer to the release notes for information regarding known issues:
Deep Learning AMI (Ubuntu) Known Issues Deep Learning AMI (Amazon Linux) Known Issues

Next Up
Running Jupyter Notebook Tutorials

Using the Deep Learning Base AMI

Using to the Deep Learning Base AMI

The Base AMI comes with a foundational platform of GPU drivers and acceleration libraries to deploy your own customized deep learning environment. By default the AMI is configured with NVidia CUDA 9 environment. However, you can also switch to a CUDA 8 environment by reconfiguring the environment variable `LD_LIBRARY_PATH`. You simply need to replace the CUDA 9 portion of the environment variable string with its CUDA 8 equivalent.

Configuring CUDA Versions

CUDA 9 portion of the LD_LIBRARY_PATH string (installed by default)

... *:/usr/local/cuda-9.0/lib64:/usr/local/cuda-9.0/extras/CUPTI/lib64:/lib/nccl/cuda-9* **:...rest of LD_LIBRARY_PATH value**

Replace with CUDA 8

... *:/usr/local/cuda-8.0/lib64:/usr/local/cuda-8.0/extras/CUPTI/lib64:/lib/nccl/cuda-8* **:...rest of LD_LIBRARY_PATH value**

Tip
Refer to the release notes for information regarding known issues:
Deep Learning Base AMI (Amazon Linux) Known IssuesDeep Learning Base AMI (Ubuntu) Known Issues

Running Jupyter Notebook Tutorials

Tutorials and examples ship with each of the deep learning projects' source and in most cases they will run on any DLAMI. If you chose the Deep Learning AMI with Conda, you get the added benefit of a few hand-picked tutorials already set up and ready to try out.

To run the Jupyter notebook tutorials installed on the DLAMI, you will need to Set up a Jupyter Notebook Server.

Once the Jupyter server is running, you can run the tutorials through your web browser. If you are running the Deep Learning AMI with Conda or if you have set up Python environments, you can switch Python kernels from the Jupyter notebook interface. Select the appropriate kernel before trying to run a framework-specific tutorial. Further examples of this are provided for users of the Deep Learning AMI with Conda.

As a quick recap of how to start up Jupyter and connect, run the following on your instance.

```
1 $ source activate python3
2 $ jupyter notebook
```

Then run the following locally on your macOS or Linux client. For Windows, see detailed instructions at Set up PuTTY.

```
1 $ ssh -i ~/mykeypair.pem -L 8157:127.0.0.1:8888 ubuntu@ec2-###-##-##-###.compute-1.amazonaws.com
```

If you want to try other tutorials, just download them to this folder and run them from Jupyter.

Note
Many tutorials require additional Python modules that may not be set up on your DLAMI. If you get an error like `"xyz module not found"`, log in to the DLAMI, activate the environment as described above, then install the necessary modules.

Tip
Deep learning tutorials and examples often rely on one or more GPUs. If your instance type doesn't have a GPU, you may need to change some of the example's code to get it to run.

Navigating the Installed Tutorials

Once you're logged in to the Jupyter server and can see the tutorials directory, you will be presented with folders of tutorials by each framework name. If you don't see a framework listed, then tutorials are not available for that framework on your current DLAMI. Click on the name of the framework to see the listed tutorials, then click a tutorial to launch it.

The first time you run a notebook on the Deep Learning AMI with Conda, it will want to know which environment you would like to use. It will prompt you to select from a list. Each environment is named according to this pattern:

`Environment (conda_framework_python-version)`

For example, you might see `Environment (conda_mxnet_p36)`, which signifies that the environment has MXNet and Python 3. The other variation of this would be `Environment (conda_mxnet_p27)`, which signifies that the environment has MXNet and Python 2.

Tip
If you're concerned about which version of CUDA is active, one way to see it is in the MOTD when you first log in to the DLAMI.

Switching Environments with Jupyter

If you decide to try a tutorial for a different framework, be sure to verify the currently running kernel. This info can be seen in the upper right of the Jupyter interface, just below the logout button. You can change the kernel on any open notebook by clicking the Jupyter menu item **Kernel**, then **Change Kernel**, and then clicking the environment that suits the notebook you're running.

At this point you'll need to rerun any cells because a change in the kernel will erase the state of anything you've run previously.

Tip
Switching between frameworks can be fun and educational, however you can run out of memory. If you start running into errors, look at the terminal window that has the Jupyter server running. There are helpful messages and error logging here, and you may see an out-of-memory error. To fix this, you can go to the home page of your Jupyter server, click the **Running** tab, then click **Shutdown** for each of the tutorials that are probably still running in the background and eating up all of your memory.

Next Up
For more examples and sample code from each framework, click **Next** or continue to Apache MXNet.

Apache MXNet

MXNet Tutorial

To activate the framework, follow these instructions on your Deep Learning AMI with Conda.

For Python 3 with CUDA 9 with cuDNN 7:

```
1 $ source activate mxnet_p36
```

For Python 2 with CUDA 9 with cuDNN 7:

```
1 $ source activate mxnet_p27
```

Start the iPython terminal.

```
1 (mxnet_p36)$ ipython
```

Run a quick MXNet program. Create a 5x5 matrix, an instance of the NDArray, with elements initialized to 0. Print the array.

```
1 import mxnet as mx
2 mx.ndarray.zeros((5,5)).asnumpy()
```

Verify the result.

```
1 array([[ 0.,   0.,   0.,   0.,   0.],
2        [ 0.,   0.,   0.,   0.,   0.],
3        [ 0.,   0.,   0.,   0.,   0.],
4        [ 0.,   0.,   0.,   0.,   0.],
5        [ 0.,   0.,   0.,   0.,   0.]], dtype=float32)
```

More Tutorials

You can find more tutorials in the Deep Learning AMI with Conda tutorials folder in the home directory of the DLAMI. Your Deep Learning AMI with Conda also comes with:

1. Running Model Server for Apache MXNet on the Deep Learning AMI with Conda

For further tutorials and examples refer to the framework's official Python docs, Python API for MXNet, and the Apache MXNet website.

Caffe2

Caffe2 Tutorial

To activate the framework, follow these instructions on your Deep Learning AMI with Conda.

There is only the Python 2 with CUDA 9 with cuDNN 7 option:

```
1 $ source activate caffe2_p27
```

Start the iPython terminal.

```
1 (caffe2_p27)$ ipython
```

Run a quick Caffe2 program.

```
1 from caffe2.python import workspace, model_helper
2 import numpy as np
3 # Create random tensor of three dimensions
4 x = np.random.rand(4, 3, 2)
5 print(x)
6 print(x.shape)
7 workspace.FeedBlob("my_x", x)
8 x2 = workspace.FetchBlob("my_x")
9 print(x2)
```

You should see the initial numpy random arrays printed and then those loaded into a Caffe2 blob. Note that after loading they are the same.

More Tutorials

For more tutorials and examples refer to the framework's official Python docs, Python API for Caffe2, and the Caffe2 website.

Chainer

Chainer is a flexible Python-based framework for easily and intuitively writing complex neural network architectures. Chainer makes it easy to use multi-GPU instances for training. Chainer also automatically logs results, graph loss and accuracy, and produces output for visualualizing the neural network with a computational graph. It is included with the Deep Learning AMI with Conda (DLAMI with Conda).

The following topics show you how to train on multiple GPUs, a single GPU, and a CPU, create visualizations, and test your Chainer installation.

- Training a Model with Chainer
- Use Chainer to Train on Multiple GPUs
- Use Chainer to Train on a Single GPU
- Use Chainer to Train with CPUs
- Graphing Results
- Testing Chainer
- More Info

Training a Model with Chainer

This tutorial shows you how to use example Chainer scripts to train a model with the MNIST dataset. MNIST is a database of handwritten numbers that is commonly used to train image recognition models. The tutorial also shows the difference in training speed between training on a CPU and one or more GPUs.

Use Chainer to Train on Multiple GPUs

To train on multiple GPUs

1. Connect to the instance running Deep Learning AMI with Conda. Refer to the Selecting the Instance Type for DLAMI or the Amazon EC2 documentation on how to select or connect to an instance.

2. Activate the Python 3 Chainer environment:

```
1 $ source activate chainer_p36
```

3. To get the latest tutorials, clone the Chainer repository, checkout Chainer version 3.5.0, and navigate to the examples folder:

```
1 (chainer_p36) :~$ cd ~/src
2 (chainer_p36) :~/src$ git clone https://github.com/chainer/chainer.git
3 (chainer_p36) :~/src$ git checkout tags/v3.5.0
4 (chainer_p36) :~/src$ cd chainer/examples/mnist
```

4. Run the example in the `train_mnist_data_parallel.py` script. By default, the script uses the GPUs running on your instance of Deep Learning AMI with Conda. The script can be run on a maximum of two GPUs. It will ignore any GPUs past the first two. It detects one or both automatically. If you are running an instance without GPUs, skip to Use Chainer to Train with CPUs, later in this tutorial.

```
1 (chainer_p36) :~/src/chainer/examples/mnist$ python train_mnist_data_parallel.py
```

While the Chainer script trains a model using the MNIST database, you see the results for each epoch.

Then you see example output as the script runs. The following example output was run on a p3.8xlarge instance. The script's output shows "GPU: 0, 1", which indicates that it is using the first two of the four available GPUs. The scripts typically use an index of GPUs starting with zero, instead of a total count.

```
1 GPU: 0, 1
2
3 # unit: 1000
4 # Minibatch-size: 400
5 # epoch: 20
6
7 epoch       main/loss    validation/main/loss   main/accuracy   validation/main/accuracy
       elapsed_time
8 1           0.277561     0.114709               0.919933        0.9654
       6.59261
9 2           0.0882352    0.0799204              0.973334        0.9752
       8.25162
10 3          0.0520674    0.0697055              0.983967        0.9786
       9.91661
11 4          0.0326329    0.0638036              0.989834        0.9805
       11.5767
12 5          0.0272191    0.0671859              0.9917          0.9796
       13.2341
13 6          0.0151008    0.0663898              0.9953          0.9813
       14.9068
14 7          0.0137765    0.0664415              0.995434        0.982
       16.5649
15 8          0.0116909    0.0737597              0.996           0.9801
       18.2176
16 9          0.00773858   0.0795216              0.997367        0.979
       19.8797
17 10         0.00705076   0.0825639              0.997634        0.9785
       21.5388
18 11         0.00773019   0.0858256              0.9978          0.9787
       23.2003
19 12         0.0120371    0.0940225              0.996034        0.9776
       24.8587
20 13         0.00906567   0.0753452              0.997033        0.9824
       26.5167
21 14         0.00852253   0.082996               0.996967        0.9812
       28.1777
22 15         0.00670928   0.102362               0.997867        0.9774
       29.8308
23 16         0.00873565   0.0691577              0.996867        0.9832
       31.498
24 17         0.00717177   0.094268               0.997767        0.9802
       33.152
25 18         0.00585393   0.0778739              0.998267        0.9827
       34.8268
26 19         0.00764773   0.107757               0.9975          0.9773
       36.4819
27 20         0.00620508   0.0834309              0.998167        0.9834
       38.1389
```

5. While your training is running it is useful to look at your GPU utilization. You can verify which GPUs are active and view their load. NVIDIA provides a tool for this, which can be run with the command `nvidia-smi`. However, it will only tell you a snapshot of the utilization, so it's more informative to combine this with the Linux command `watch`. The following command will use `watch` with `nvidia-smi` to refresh the current GPU utilization every tenth of a second. Open up another terminal session to your DLAMI, and run the following command:

```
1 (chainer_p36) :~$ watch -n0.1 nvidia-smi
```

You will see an output similar to the following result. Use `ctrl-c` to close the tool, or just keep it running while you try out other examples in your first terminal session.

```
1 Every 0.1s: nvidia-smi                                 Wed Feb 28 00:28:50 2018
2
3 Wed Feb 28 00:28:50 2018
4 +-----------------------------------------------------------------------------+
5 | NVIDIA-SMI 384.111                 Driver Version: 384.111                  |
6 |-------------------------------+----------------------+----------------------+
7 | GPU  Name        Persistence-M| Bus-Id        Disp.A | Volatile Uncorr. ECC |
8 | Fan  Temp  Perf  Pwr:Usage/Cap|         Memory-Usage | GPU-Util  Compute M. |
9 |===============================+======================+======================|
10 |   0  Tesla V100-SXM2...  On   | 00000000:00:1B.0 Off |                    0 |
11 | N/A   46C    P0    56W / 300W |    728MiB / 16152MiB |     10%      Default |
12 +-------------------------------+----------------------+----------------------+
13 |   1  Tesla V100-SXM2...  On   | 00000000:00:1C.0 Off |                    0 |
14 | N/A   44C    P0    53W / 300W |    696MiB / 16152MiB |      4%      Default |
15 +-------------------------------+----------------------+----------------------+
16 |   2  Tesla V100-SXM2...  On   | 00000000:00:1D.0 Off |                    0 |
17 | N/A   42C    P0    38W / 300W |     10MiB / 16152MiB |      0%      Default |
18 +-------------------------------+----------------------+----------------------+
19 |   3  Tesla V100-SXM2...  On   | 00000000:00:1E.0 Off |                    0 |
20 | N/A   46C    P0    40W / 300W |     10MiB / 16152MiB |      0%      Default |
21 +-------------------------------+----------------------+----------------------+
22
23 +-----------------------------------------------------------------------------+
24 | Processes:                                                       GPU Memory |
25 | GPU       PID   Type   Process name                              Usage      |
26 |=============================================================================|
27 |   0     54418      C   python                                        718MiB |
28 |   1     54418      C   python                                        686MiB |
29 +-----------------------------------------------------------------------------+
```

In this example, GPU 0 and GPU 1 are active, and GPU 2 and 3 are not. You can also see memory utilization per GPU.

6. As training completes, note the elapsed time in your first terminal session. In the example, elapsed time is 38.1389 seconds.

Use Chainer to Train on a Single GPU

This example shows how to train on a single GPU. You might do this if you have only one GPU available or just to see how multi-GPU training might scale with Chainer.

To use Chainer to train on a single GPU

- For this example, you use another script, `train_mnist.py`, and tell it to use just GPU 0 with the **--gpu=0** argument. To see how a different GPUs activate in the `nvidia-smi` console, you can tell the script to use GPU number 1 by using **--gpu=1** .

```
1 (chainer_p36) :~/src/chainer/examples/mnist$ python train_mnist.py --gpu=0
```

```
1 GPU: 0
2 # unit: 1000
```

```
3 # Minibatch-size: 100
4 # epoch: 20
5
6 epoch     main/loss    validation/main/loss   main/accuracy   validation/main/accuracy
          elapsed_time
7 1          0.192348    0.0909235              0.940934        0.9719
          5.3861
8 2          0.0746767   0.069854               0.976566        0.9785
          8.97146
9 3          0.0477152   0.0780836              0.984982        0.976
          12.5596
10 4         0.0347092   0.0701098              0.988498        0.9783
          16.1577
11 5         0.0263807   0.08851                0.991515        0.9793
          19.7939
12 6         0.0253418   0.0945821              0.991599        0.9761
          23.4643
13 7         0.0209954   0.0683193              0.993398        0.981
          27.0317
14 8         0.0179036   0.080285               0.994149        0.9819
          30.6325
15 9         0.0183184   0.0690474              0.994198        0.9823
          34.2469
16 10        0.0127616   0.0776328              0.996165        0.9814
          37.8693
17 11        0.0145421   0.0970157              0.995365        0.9801
          41.4629
18 12        0.0129053   0.0922671              0.995899        0.981
          45.0233
19 13        0.0135988   0.0717195              0.995749        0.9857
          48.6271
20 14        0.00898215  0.0840777              0.997216        0.9839
          52.2269
21 15        0.0103909   0.123506               0.996832        0.9771
          55.8667
22 16        0.012099    0.0826434              0.996616        0.9847
          59.5001
23 17        0.0066183   0.101969               0.997999        0.9826
          63.1294
24 18        0.00989864  0.0877713              0.997116        0.9829
          66.7449
25 19        0.0101816   0.0972672              0.996966        0.9822
          70.3686
26 20        0.00833862  0.0899327              0.997649        0.9835
          74.0063
```

In this example, running on a single GPU took almost twice as long! Training larger models or larger datasets will yield different results from this example, so experiment to further evaluate GPU performance.

Use Chainer to Train with CPUs

Now try training on a CPU-only mode. Run the same script, `python train_mnist.py`, without arguments:

```
1 (chainer_p36) :~/src/chainer/examples/mnist$ python train_mnist.py
```

In the output, GPU: -1 indicates that no GPU is used:

```
1 GPU: -1
2 # unit: 1000
3 # Minibatch-size: 100
4 # epoch: 20
5
6 epoch       main/loss    validation/main/loss  main/accuracy   validation/main/accuracy
      elapsed_time
```

epoch	main/loss	validation/main/loss	main/accuracy	validation/main/accuracy	elapsed_time
1	0.192083	0.0918663	0.94195	0.9712	11.2661
2	0.0732366	0.0790055	0.977267	0.9747	23.9823
3	0.0485948	0.0723766	0.9844	0.9787	37.5275
4	0.0352731	0.0817955	0.987967	0.9772	51.6394
5	0.029566	0.0807774	0.990217	0.9764	65.2657
6	0.025517	0.0678703	0.9915	0.9814	79.1276
7	0.0194185	0.0716576	0.99355	0.9808	93.8085
8	0.0174553	0.0786768	0.994217	0.9809	108.648
9	0.0148924	0.0923396	0.994983	0.9791	123.737
10	0.018051	0.099924	0.99445	0.9791	139.483
11	0.014241	0.0860133	0.995783	0.9806	156.132
12	0.0124222	0.0829303	0.995967	0.9822	173.173
13	0.00846336	0.122346	0.997133	0.9769	190.365
14	0.011392	0.0982324	0.996383	0.9803	207.746
15	0.0113111	0.0985907	0.996533	0.9813	225.764
16	0.0114328	0.0905778	0.996483	0.9811	244.258
17	0.00900945	0.0907504	0.9974	0.9825	263.379
18	0.0130028	0.0917099	0.996217	0.9831	282.887
19	0.00950412	0.0850664	0.997133	0.9839	303.113
20	0.00808573	0.112367	0.998067	0.9778	323.852

In this example, MNIST was trained in 323 seconds, which is more than 11x longer than training with two GPUs. If you've ever doubted the power of GPUs, this example shows how much more efficient they are.

Graphing Results

Chainer also automatically logs results, graph loss and accuracy, and produces output for plotting the computational graph.

To generate the computational graph

1. After any training run finishes, you may navigate to the **result** directory and view the run's accuracy and loss in the form of two automatically generated images. Navigate there now, and list the contents:

```
1 (chainer_p36) :~/src/chainer/examples/mnist$ cd result
2 (chainer_p36) :~/src/chainer/examples/mnist/result$ ls
```

The **result** directory contains two files in .png format: accuracy.png and loss.png.

2. To generate the computational graph, run the following command:

```
1 (chainer_p36) :~/src/chainer/examples/mnist/result$ dot -Tpng mnist_result/cg.dot -o
    mnist_result/cg.png
```

3. To view the graphs, use the **scp** command to copy them to your local computer.

In a macOS terminal, running the following **scp** command downloads all three files to your Downloads folder. Replace the placeholders for the location of the key file and server address with your information. For other operating systems, use the appropriate **scp** command format.

```
1 (chainer_p36) :~/src/chainer/examples/mnist/result$ scp -i "your-key-file.pem" ubuntu@your-
    dlami-address.compute-1.amazonaws.com:~/src/chainer/examples/mnist/result/*.png ~/
    Downloads
```

The following images are examples of accuracy, loss, and computational graphs, respectively.

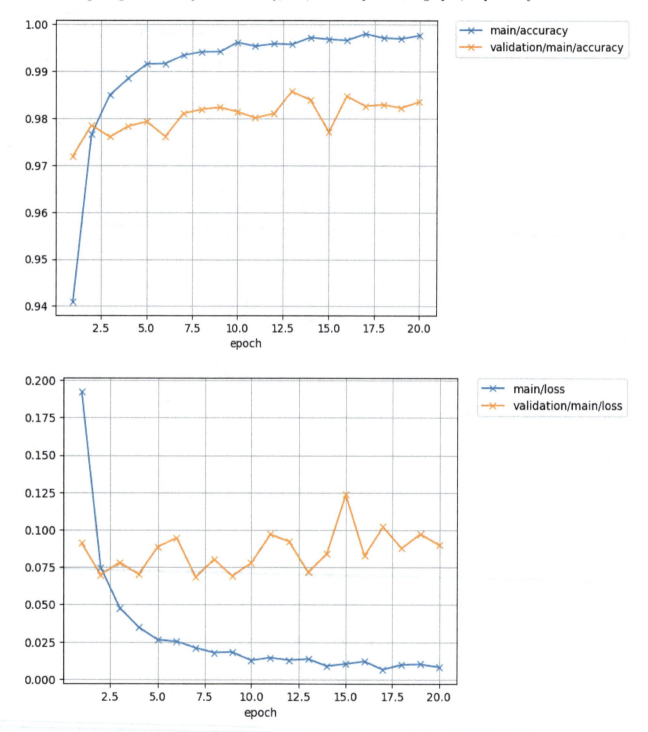

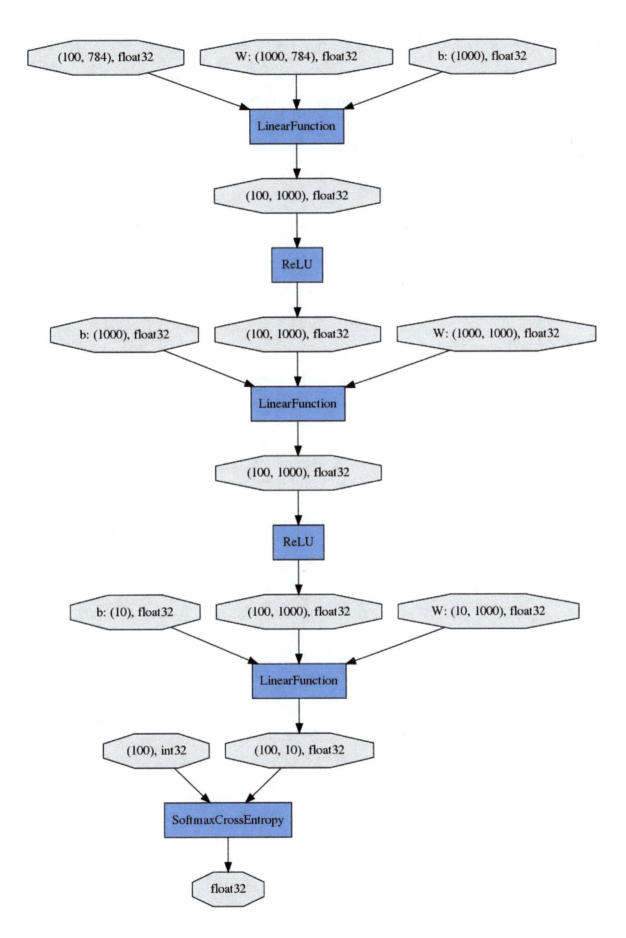

Testing Chainer

To test Chainer and verify GPU support with a preinstalled test script, run the following command:

```
1  (chainer_p36) :~/src/chainer/examples/mnist/result$ cd ~/src/bin
2  (chainer_p36) :~/src/bin$ ./testChainer
```

This downloads Chainer source code and runs the Chainer multi-GPU MNIST example.

More Info

To learn more about Chainer, see the Chainer documentation website. The `Chainer` examples folder contains more examples. Try them to see how they perform.

CNTK

CNTK Tutorial

To activate the framework, follow these instructions on your Deep Learning AMI with Conda.

For Python 3 with CUDA 9 with cuDNN 7:

```
1 $ source activate cntk_p36
```

For Python 2 with CUDA 9 with cuDNN 7:

```
1 $ source activate cntk_p27
```

Start the iPython terminal.

```
1 (caffe2_p27)$ ipython
```

Run a quick CNTK program.

```
1 import cntk as C
2 C.__version__
3 c = C.constant(3, shape=(2,3))
4 c.asarray()
```

You should see the CNTK version, then the output of a 2x3 array of 3's.

If you have a GPU instance, you can test it with the following code example. A result of **True** is what you would expect if CNTK can access the GPU.

```
1 from cntk.device import try_set_default_device, gpu
2 try_set_default_device(gpu(0))
```

More Tutorials

For more tutorials and examples refer to the framework's official Python docs, Python API for CNTK, and the CNTK website.

Keras

Keras Tutorial

To activate the framework, follow these instructions on your Deep Learning AMI with Conda.

For Keras 1 with a MXNet backend on Python 3 with CUDA 9 with cuDNN 7:

```
1 $ source activate mxnet_p36
```

For Keras 1 with a MXNet backend on Python 2 with CUDA 9 with cuDNN 7:

```
1 $ source activate mxnet_p27
```

For Keras 2 with a TensorFlow backend on Python 3 with CUDA 9 with cuDNN 7:

```
1 $ source activate tensorflow_p36
```

For Keras 2 with a TensorFlow backend on Python 2 with CUDA 9 with cuDNN 7:

```
1 $ source activate tensorflow_p27
```

More Tutorials

You can find more tutorials in the Deep Learning AMI with Conda tutorials/tensorflow folder in the home directory of the DLAMI. For additional tutorials and examples, see the Keras website.

PyTorch

PyTorch Tutorial

To activate the framework, follow these instructions on your Deep Learning AMI with Conda.

For Python 3 with CUDA 9 with cuDNN 7:

```
1 $ source activate pytorch_p36
```

For Python 2 with CUDA 9 with cuDNN 7:

```
1 $ source activate pytorch_p27
```

Start the iPython terminal.

```
1 (pytorch_p36)$ ipython
```

Run a quick PyTorch program.

```
1 import torch
2 x = torch.rand(5, 3)
3 print(x)
4 print(x.size())
5 y = torch.rand(5, 3)
6 print(torch.add(x, y))
```

You should see the initial random array printed, then its size, and then the addition of another random array.

More Tutorials

You can find more tutorials in the Deep Learning AMI with Conda tutorials folder in the home directory of the DLAMI. For further tutorials and examples refer to the framework's official docs, PyTorch documentation, and the PyTorch website.

TensorFlow

This tutorial shows how to activate TensorFlow on an instance running the Deep Learning AMI with Conda (DLAMI on Conda) and run a TensorFlow program.

To run TensorFlow on the DLAMI with Conda

1. To activate TensorFlow, open an Amazon Elastic Compute Cloud (Amazon EC2) instance of the DLAMI with Conda.

   - For TensorFlow + Keras 2 on Python 3 with CUDA 8, run this command:

   ```
   1 $ source activate tensorflow_p36
   ```

   - For TensorFlow + Keras 2 on Python 2 with CUDA 8, run this command:

   ```
   1 $ source activate tensorflow_p27
   ```

2. Start the iPython terminal:

   ```
   1 (tensorflow_p36)$ ipython
   ```

3. Run a TensorFlow program to verify that it is working properly:

   ```
   1 import tensorflow as tf
   2 hello = tf.constant('Hello, TensorFlow!')
   3 sess = tf.Session()
   4 print(sess.run(hello))
   ```

   `Hello, TensorFlow!` should appear on your screen.

More Info

TensorBoard

TensorFlow Serving

For tutorials, see the folder called `Deep Learning AMI with Conda tutorials`in the home directory of the DLAMI.

For even more tutorials and examples, see the TensorFlow documentation for the TensorFlow Python API, and visit the TensorFlow website.

Theano

Theano Tutorial

To activate the framework, follow these instructions on your Deep Learning AMI with Conda.

For Theano + Keras in Python 3 with CUDA 9 with cuDNN 7:

```
1 $ source activate theano_p36
```

For Theano + Keras in Python 2 with CUDA 9 with cuDNN 7:

```
1 $ source activate theano_p27
```

Start the iPython terminal.

```
1 (theano_p36)$ ipython
```

Run a quick Theano program.

```
1 import numpy
2 import theano
3 import theano.tensor as T
4 from theano import pp
5 x = T.dscalar('x')
6 y = x ** 2
7 gy = T.grad(y, x)
8 pp(gy)
```

You should see Theano computing a symbolic gradient.

More Tutorials

For further tutorials and examples refer to the framework's official docs, Theano Python API, and the Theano website.

Running Model Server for Apache MXNet on the Deep Learning AMI with Conda

Model Server for Apache MXNet (MMS)is a flexible tool for serving deep learning models that have been exported from Apache MXNet. MMS comes preinstalled with the DLAMI with Conda. This tutorial for MMS will demonstrate how to serve an image classification model, and guide you to finding a Single Shot Detector (SSD) example that is included on the DLAMI with Conda.

- Serve an Image Classification Model on MMS
- Serve an SSD Model on MMS
- More Info

Serve an Image Classification Model on MMS

This tutorial shows how to serve an image classification model with MMS. The model is provided via the MMS Model Zoo, and is automatically downloaded when you start MMS. Once the server is running, it listens for prediction requests. When you upload an image, in this case, an image of a kitten, the server returns a prediction of the top 5 matching classes out of the 1,000 classes that the model was trained on. More information on the models, how they were trained, and how to test them can be found in the MMS Model Zoo.

To serve an example image classification model on MMS

1. Connect to an Amazon Elastic Compute Cloud (Amazon EC2) instance of the Deep Learning AMI with Conda.

2. Activate an MXNet environment:

```
1 $ source activate mxnet_p36
```

3. Run MMS with the following command. This command also downloads the model and serves it.

```
1 $ mxnet-model-server \
2 --models squeezenet=https://s3.amazonaws.com/model-server/models/squeezenet_v1.1/
    squeezenet_v1.1.model
```

MMS is now running on your host, and is listening for inference requests.

4. To test MMS, in a new terminal window, connect to the instance that is running the DLAMI.

5. Download an image of a kitten and send it to the MMS predict endpoint:

```
1 $ curl -O https://s3.amazonaws.com/model-server/inputs/kitten.jpg
2 $ curl -X POST http://127.0.0.1:8080/squeezenet/predict -F "data=@kitten.jpg"
```

The predict endpoint returns a prediction in JSON similar to the following top five predictions, where the image has a 94% probability of containing an Egyption cat, followed by a 5.5% chance it has a lynx or catamount:

```
1      {
2      "prediction": [
3      [
4      {
5      "class": "n02124075 Egyptian cat",
6      "probability": 0.940
7      },
8      {
9      "class": "n02127052 lynx, catamount",
10     "probability": 0.055
```

```
11          },
12          {
13          "class": "n02123045 tabby, tabby cat",
14          "probability": 0.002
15          },
16          {
17          "class": "n02123159 tiger cat",
18          "probability": 0.0003
19          },
20          {
21          "class": "n02123394 Persian cat",
22          "probability": 0.0002          }
23          ]
24          ]
25          }
```

This tutorial focuses on basic model serving. When you're ready to learn more about other MMS features, see the MMS documentation on GitHub.

Serve an SSD Model on MMS

The DLAMI with Conda includes an example application that uses MMS to serve a Single Shot Detection (SSD) model. To see the example, open the DLAMI in a terminal, and navigate to the `~/tutorials/MXNet-Model-Server/ssd` folder. For instructions on running the example, see the `README.md` file or the latest version of the example in the MMS GitHub repository.

More Info

For more MMS examples—such as examples of exporting models and setting up MMS with Docker—or to take advantage of the latest MMS features, star the MMS project page on GitHub.

TensorFlow Serving

TensorFlow Serving is a flexible, high-performance serving system for machine learning models.

Train and Serve an MNIST Model with TensorFlow Serving

The `tensorflow-serving-api` is pre-installed with Deep Learning AMI with Conda! You will find an example scripts to train, export, and serve an MNIST model in `~/tutorials/TensorFlow/serving`. For this tutorial we will export a model then serve it with the `tensorflow_model_server` application. Finally, you can test the model server with an example client script.

First, connect to your Deep Learning AMI with Conda and activate the Python 2.7 TensorFlow environmenent. The example scripts are not compatible with Python 3.x.

```
1 $ source activate tensorflow_p27
```

Now change directories to the serving example scripts folder.

```
1 $ cd ~/tutorials/TensorFlow/serving
```

Run the script that will train and export an MNIST model. As the script's only argument, you need to provide a folder location for it to save the model. For now we can just put it in `mnist_model`. The script will create the folder for you.

```
1 $ python mnist_saved_model.py /tmp/mnist_model
```

Be patient, as this script may take a while before providing any output. When the training is complete and the model is finally exported you should see the following:

```
1          Done training!
2          Exporting trained model to mnist_model/1
3          Done exporting!
```

Your next step is to run `tensorflow_model_server` to serve the exported model.

```
1 $ tensorflow_model_server --port=9000 --model_name=mnist --model_base_path=/tmp/mnist_model
```

A client script is provided for you to test the server.

To test it out, you will need to open a new terminal window.

```
1 $ python mnist_client.py --num_tests=1000 --server=localhost:9000
```

More Features and Examples

If you are interested in learning more about TensorFlow Serving, check out the TensorFlow website.

TensorBoard

TensorBoard lets you to visually inspect and interpret your TensorFlow runs and graphs. It runs a web server that serves a webpage for viewing and interacting with the TensorBoard visualizations.

TensorFlow and TensorBoard are preinstalled with the Deep Learning AMI with Conda (DLAMI with Conda). The DLAMI with Conda also includes an example script that uses TensorFlow to train an MNIST model with extra logging features enabled. MNIST is a database of handwritten numbers that is commonly used to train image recognition models. In this tutorial, you use the script to train an MNIST model, and TensorBoard and the logs to create visualizations.

- Train an MNIST Model and Visualize the Training with TensorBoard
- More Info

Train an MNIST Model and Visualize the Training with TensorBoard

Visualize MNIST model training with TensorBoard

1. Connect to your Amazon Elastic Compute Cloud (Amazon EC2) instance of the DLAMI with Conda.

2. Activate the Python 2.7 TensorFlow environment and navigate to the directory that contains the folder with the TensorBoard example scripts:

```
1 $ source activate tensorflow_p27
2 $ cd ~/tutorials/TensorFlow/board
```

3. Run the script that trains an MNIST model with extended logging enabled:

```
1 $ python mnist_with_summaries.py
```

The script writes the logs to /tmp/tensorflow/mnist.

4. Pass the location of the logs to tensorboard:

```
1 $ tensorboard --logdir=/tmp/tensorflow/mnist
```

TensorBoard launches the visualization web server on port 6006.

5. For easy access from your local browser, you can change the web server port to port 80 or another port. Whichever port you use, you will need to open this port in the EC2 security group for your DLAMI. You can also use port forwarding. For instructions on changing your security group settings and port forwarding, see Set up a Jupyter Notebook Server. The default settings are described in the next step. **Note** If you need to run both Jupyter server and a TensorBoard server, use a different port for each.

6. Open port 6006 (or the port you assigned to the visualization web server) on your EC2 instance.

   1. Open your EC2 instance in the Amazon EC2console at https://console.aws.amazon.com/ec2/.

   2. In the Amazon EC2 console, choose **Network & Security**, then choose**Security Groups**.

   3. For **Security Group**, , choose the one that was created most recently (see the timestamp in the description).

   4. Choose the **Inbound** tab, and choose **Edit**.

   5. Choose **Add Rule**.

   6. In the new row, type the followings:

      Type : Custom **TCP Rule**

      Protocol: TCP

Port Range: **6006** (or the port that you assigned to the visualization server)

Source: **Anywhere (0.0.0.0/0,::/0)**

7. Open the web page for the TensorBoard visualizations by using the public IP or DNS address of the EC2 instance that's running the DLAMI with Conda and the port that you opened for TensorBoard:

http:// *YourInstancePublicDNS***:6006**

More Info

To learn more about TensorBoard, see the TensorBoard website.

10 Minute Tutorials

- Launch a AWS Deep Learning AMI (in 10 minutes)

Resources and Support

- Forums
- Related Blog Posts
- FAQ

Forums

- Forum: AWS Deep Learning AMIs

Related Blog Posts

- Updated List of Articles Related to Deep Learning AMIs

- Launch a AWS Deep Learning AMI (in 10 minutes)

- Faster Training with Optimized TensorFlow 1.6 on Amazon EC2 C5 and P3 Instances

- New AWS Deep Learning AMIs for Machine Learning Practitioners

- New Training Courses Available: Introduction to Machine Learning & Deep Learning on AWS

- Journey into Deep Learning with AWS

FAQ

- **Q.** How do I keep track of product announcements related to DLAMI?

  Here are two suggestions for this:

  - Bookmark this blog category, "AWS Deep Learning AMIs" found here: Updated List of Articles Related to Deep Learning AMIs.

  - "Watch" the Forum: AWS Deep Learning AMIs

- **Q.** Are the NVIDIA drivers and CUDA installed?

  Yes. Some DLAMIs have different versions. The Deep Learning AMI with Conda has the most recent versions of any DLAMI. This is covered in more detail in CUDA Installations and Framework Bindings. You can also refer to the specific AMI's detail page on the marketplace to confirm what is installed.

- **Q.** Is cuDNN installed?

  Yes.

- **Q.** How do I see that the GPUs are detected and their current status?

  Run `nvidia-smi`. This will show one or more GPUs, depending on the instance type, along with their current memory consumption.

- **Q.** Are virtual environments set up for me?

  Yes, but only on the Deep Learning AMI with Conda.

- **Q.** What version of Python is installed?

  Each DLAMI has both Python 2 and 3. The Deep Learning AMI with Conda have environments for both versions for each framework. The Deep Learning AMI with Source Code has the deep learning frameworks installed into specific Python versions, denoted with "2" or "3" in the folder names.

- **Q.** Is Keras installed?

  This depends on the AMI. The Deep Learning AMI with Conda has Keras available as a front end for each framework. The version of Keras depends on the framework's support for it.

- **Q.** Is it free?

  All of the DLAMIs are free. However, depending on the instance type you choose, the instance may not be free. See Pricing for the DLAMI for more info.

- **Q.** I'm getting CUDA errors or GPU-related messages from my framework. What's wrong?

  Check what instance type you used. It needs to have a GPU for many examples and tutorials to work. If running `nvidia-smi` shows no GPU, then you need to spin up another DLAMI using an instance with one or more GPUs. See Selecting the Instance Type for DLAMI for more info.

- **Q.** Can I use Docker?

  Docker is not installed, but you can install it and use it. Note that you will want to use nvidia-docker on GPU instances to make use of the GPU. In this situation, a AWS Deep Learning AMI, Ubuntu Versions is your best choice, as there are currently some incompatibilities with nvidia-docker and the Deep Learning AMI (Amazon Linux).

- **Q.** What regions are Linux DLAMIs available in?
  [See the AWS documentation website for more details]

- **Q.** What regions are Windows DLAMIs available in?
  [See the AWS documentation website for more details]

Appendix

- AMI Options
- DLAMI: Release Notes

AMI Options

The following topics describe the categories of AWS Deep Learning AMIs.

- Deep Learning AMI with Conda
- Deep Learning Base AMI
- Deep Learning AMI with Source Code
- Deep Learning AMI with CUDA 9
- Deep Learning AMI with CUDA 8
- AWS Deep Learning AMI, Ubuntu Versions
- AWS Deep Learning AMI, Amazon Linux Versions
- AWS Deep Learning AMI, Windows Versions

Deep Learning AMI with CUDA 9

Use the Launching and Configuring a DLAMI guide to continue with one of these DLAMI.

- Deep Learning AMI (Ubuntu)
- Deep Learning AMI (Amazon Linux)
- Deep Learning Base AMI (Ubuntu)
- Deep Learning Base AMI (Amazon Linux)
- Deep Learning AMI with Source Code (CUDA 9, Ubuntu)
- Deep Learning AMI with Source Code (CUDA 9, Amazon Linux)
- Deep Learning AMI (Windows 2012 R2)
- Deep Learning AMI (Windows 2016)

Note

The Deep Learning AMI with Conda have both CUDA 8 and CUDA 9. The frameworks will use the latest CUDA that they support.

The Deep Learning Base AMI also have both CUDA 8 and CUDA 9. To switch between the two, follow the directions on Using the Deep Learning Base AMI.

Deep Learning AMI with CUDA 8

Use the Launching and Configuring a DLAMI guide to continue with one of these DLAMI.

- Deep Learning AMI (Ubuntu)
- Deep Learning AMI (Amazon Linux)
- Deep Learning Base AMI (Ubuntu)
- Deep Learning Base AMI (Amazon Linux)
- Deep Learning AMI with Source Code (CUDA 8, Ubuntu)
- Deep Learning AMI with Source Code (CUDA 8, Amazon Linux)
- Deep Learning AMI (Windows 2012 R2)
- Deep Learning AMI (Windows 2016)

Note

The Deep Learning AMI with Conda have both CUDA 8 and CUDA 9. The frameworks will use the latest CUDA that they support.

The Deep Learning Base AMI also have both CUDA 8 and CUDA 9. To switch between the two, follow the directions on Using the Deep Learning Base AMI.

AWS Deep Learning AMI, Ubuntu Versions

Use the Launching and Configuring a DLAMI guide to continue with one of these DLAMI.

- Deep Learning AMI (Ubuntu)

- Deep Learning Base AMI (Ubuntu)

- Deep Learning AMI with Source Code (CUDA 9, Ubuntu)

- Deep Learning AMI with Source Code (CUDA 8, Ubuntu)

These DLAMIs are available in these regions:

Region	Code
US East (Ohio)	ec2-us-east-2
US East (N. Virginia)	ec2-us-east-1
US West (N. California)	ec2-us-west-1
US West (Oregon)	ec2-us-west-2
Beijing (China)	cn-north-1
Asia Pacific (Mumbai)	ec2-ap-south-1
Asia Pacific (Seoul)	ec2-ap-northeast-2
Asia Pacific (Singapore)	ec2-ap-southeast-1
Asia Pacific (Sydney)	ec2-ap-southeast-2
Asia Pacific (Tokyo)	ec2-ap-northeast-1
Canada (Central)	ec2-ca-central-1
EU (Frankfurt)	ec2-eu-central-1
EU (Ireland)	ec2-eu-west-1
EU (London)	ec2-eu-west-2
EU (Paris)	ec2-eu-west-3
SA (Sao Paulo)	ec2-sa-east-1

AWS Deep Learning AMI, Amazon Linux Versions

Use the Launching and Configuring a DLAMI guide to continue with one of these DLAMI.

- Deep Learning AMI (Amazon Linux)
- Deep Learning Base AMI (Amazon Linux)
- Deep Learning AMI with Source Code (CUDA 9, Amazon Linux)
- Deep Learning AMI with Source Code (CUDA 8, Amazon Linux)

These DLAMIs are available in these regions:

Region	Code
US East (Ohio)	ec2-us-east-2
US East (N. Virginia)	ec2-us-east-1
US West (N. California)	ec2-us-west-1
US West (Oregon)	ec2-us-west-2
Beijing (China)	cn-north-1
Asia Pacific (Mumbai)	ec2-ap-south-1
Asia Pacific (Seoul)	ec2-ap-northeast-2
Asia Pacific (Singapore)	ec2-ap-southeast-1
Asia Pacific (Sydney)	ec2-ap-southeast-2
Asia Pacific (Tokyo)	ec2-ap-northeast-1
Canada (Central)	ec2-ca-central-1
EU (Frankfurt)	ec2-eu-central-1
EU (Ireland)	ec2-eu-west-1
EU (London)	ec2-eu-west-2
EU (Paris)	ec2-eu-west-3
SA (Sao Paulo)	ec2-sa-east-1

AWS Deep Learning AMI, Windows Versions

Use the Launching and Configuring a DLAMI guide to continue with one of these DLAMI.

- Deep Learning AMI (Windows 2016)
- Deep Learning AMI (Windows 2012 R2)

Windows DLAMIs are available in these regions:

Region	Code
US East (Ohio)	ec2-us-east-2
US East (N. Virginia)	ec2-us-east-1
GovCloud	ec2-us-gov-west-1
US West (N. California)	ec2-us-west-1
US West (Oregon)	ec2-us-west-2
Beijing (China)	cn-north-1
Asia Pacific (Mumbai)	ec2-ap-south-1
Asia Pacific (Seoul)	ec2-ap-northeast-2
Asia Pacific (Singapore)	ec2-ap-southeast-1
Asia Pacific (Sydney)	ec2-ap-southeast-2
Asia Pacific (Tokyo)	ec2-ap-northeast-1
Canada (Central)	ec2-ca-central-1
EU (Frankfurt)	ec2-eu-central-1
EU (Ireland)	ec2-eu-west-1
EU (London)	ec2-eu-west-2
SA (Sao Paulo)	ec2-sa-east-1

DLAMI: Release Notes

- Current AWS Deep Learning AMI Release Notes
- AWS Deep Learning AMI Release Archive

AWS Deep Learning AMI Release Archive

- AWS Deep Learning AMI Base Release Archive
- AWS Deep Learning AMI Conda Release Archive
- AWS Deep Learning AMI Source Release Archive
- AWS Deep Learning AMI Windows Release Archive

AWS Deep Learning AMI Base Release Archive

- Release Note Details for Deep Learning Base AMI (Amazon Linux) Version 2.0
- Release Note Details for Deep Learning Base AMI (Ubuntu) Version 2.0
- Release Note Details for Deep Learning Base AMI (Amazon Linux) Version 1.0
- Release Note Details for Deep Learning Base AMI (Ubuntu) Version 1.0

Release Note Details for Deep Learning Base AMI (Amazon Linux) Version 2.0

AWS Deep Learning AMI

The Deep Learning Base AMI are prebuilt with CUDA 8 and 9 and ready for your custom deep learning setup. The Deep Learning Base AMI uses the Anaconda Platform with both Python2 and Python3.

Highlights of the Release

1. Used Amazon Linux 2017.09 (ami-8c1be5f6) as the base AMI
2. CUDA 9
3. CuDNN 7
4. NCCL 2.1
5. CuBLAS 8 and 9
6. glibc 2.18
7. OpenCV 3.2.0

Python 2.7 and Python 3.5 Support

Python 2.7 and Python 3.6 are supported in the AMI.

CPU Instance Type Support

The AMI supports CPU Instance Types.

GPU Drivers Installed

- Nvidia 384.81
- CUDA 9.0
- CuDNN 7

Launching Deep Learning Instance

Choose the flavor of the AMI from the list below in the region of your choice and follow the steps at:
AWS Deep Learning AMI Developer Guide

Deep Learning AMI (Amazon Linux)

Available in the following regions:

Region	Code
US East (Ohio)	ec2-us-east-2

Region	Code
US East (N. Virginia)	ec2-us-east-1
US West (N. California)	ec2-us-west-1
US West (Oregon)	ec2-us-west-2
Beijing (China)	cn-north-1
Asia Pacific (Mumbai)	ec2-ap-south-1
Asia Pacific (Seoul)	ec2-ap-northeast-2
Asia Pacific (Singapore)	ec2-ap-southeast-1
Asia Pacific (Sydney)	ec2-ap-southeast-2
Asia Pacific (Tokyo)	ec2-ap-northeast-1
Canada (Central)	ec2-ca-central-1
EU (Frankfurt)	ec2-eu-central-1
EU (Ireland)	ec2-eu-west-1
EU (London)	ec2-eu-west-2
EU (Paris)	ec2-eu-west-3
SA (Sao Paulo)	ec2-sa-east-1

Test Environments

- Built on p2.16xlarge.
- Also tested on p2.xlarge, c4.4xlarge.

Known Issues

- No known issues.

Release Note Details for Deep Learning Base AMI (Ubuntu) Version 2.0

AWS Deep Learning AMI

The Deep Learning Base AMI are prebuilt with CUDA 8 and 9 and ready for your custom deep learning setup. The Deep Learning Base AMI uses the Anaconda Platform with both Python2 and Python3.

Highlights of the Release

1. Used Ubuntu 2017.09 (ami-8c1be5f6) as the base AMI
2. CUDA 9
3. CuDNN 7
4. NCCL 2.1
5. CuBLAS 8 and 9
6. glibc 2.18
7. OpenCV 3.2.0

Python 2.7 and Python 3.5 Support

Python 2.7 and Python 3.6 are supported in the AMI.

CPU Instance Type Support

The AMI supports CPU Instance Types.

GPU Drivers Installed

- Nvidia 384.81
- CUDA 9
- CuDNN 7

Launching Deep Learning Instance

Choose the flavor of the AMI from the list below in the region of your choice and follow the steps at:

AWS Deep Learning AMI Developer Guide

Deep Learning AMI (Ubuntu)

Available in the following regions:

Region	Code
US East (Ohio)	ec2-us-east-2

Region	Code
US East (N. Virginia)	ec2-us-east-1
US West (N. California)	ec2-us-west-1
US West (Oregon)	ec2-us-west-2
Beijing (China)	cn-north-1
Asia Pacific (Mumbai)	ec2-ap-south-1
Asia Pacific (Seoul)	ec2-ap-northeast-2
Asia Pacific (Singapore)	ec2-ap-southeast-1
Asia Pacific (Sydney)	ec2-ap-southeast-2
Asia Pacific (Tokyo)	ec2-ap-northeast-1
Canada (Central)	ec2-ca-central-1
EU (Frankfurt)	ec2-eu-central-1
EU (Ireland)	ec2-eu-west-1
EU (London)	ec2-eu-west-2
EU (Paris)	ec2-eu-west-3
SA (Sao Paulo)	ec2-sa-east-1

Test Environments

- Built on p2.16xlarge.
- Also tested on p2.xlarge, c4.4xlarge.

Known Issues

- No known issues.

Release Note Details for Deep Learning Base AMI (Amazon Linux) Version 1.0

AWS Deep Learning AMI

The Deep Learning Base AMI are prebuilt with CUDA 8 and 9 and ready for your custom deep learning setup. The Deep Learning Base AMI uses the Anaconda Platform with both Python2 and Python3.

Highlights of the Release

1. Used Amazon Linux 2017.09 (ami-8c1be5f6) as the base AMI
2. CUDA 9
3. CuDNN 7
4. NCCL 2.0.5
5. CuBLAS 8 and 9
6. glibc 2.18
7. OpenCV 3.2.0

Python 2.7 and Python 3.5 Support

Python 2.7 and Python 3.6 are supported in the AMI.

CPU Instance Type Support

The AMI supports CPU Instance Types.

GPU Drivers Installed

- Nvidia 384.81
- CUDA 9.0
- CuDNN 7

Launching Deep Learning Instance

Choose the flavor of the AMI from the list below in the region of your choice and follow the steps at:
AWS Deep Learning AMI Developer Guide

Deep Learning AMI (Amazon Linux)

This AMI is available in the following regions:
- US East (Ohio): ec2-us-east-2
- US East (N. Virginia): ec2-us-east-1

- US West (N. California): ec2-us-west-1

- US West (Oregon): ec2-us-west-2

- Asia Pacific (Seoul): ec2-ap-northeast-2

- Asia Pacific (Singapore): ec2-ap-southeast-1

- Asia Pacific (Tokyo): ec2-ap-northeast-1

- EU (Ireland): ec2-eu-west-1

Test Environments

- Built on p2.16xlarge.

- Also tested on p2.xlarge, c4.4xlarge.

Deep Learning Base AMI (Amazon Linux) Known Issues

- **Issue**: Versions of pip and Python are not compatible for the Amazon Linux Deep Learning AMI (DLAMI), specifically pip, which is expected to install Python 2 bindings, but instead installs Python 3 bindings.

  This is a known problem documented on the pip website. A future release will address this issue.

  Workaround: Use the relevant command below to install the package for the appropriate Python version:

  python2.7 -m pip install *some-python-package*

  python3.4 -m pip install *some-python-package*

- **Issue**: The MOTD has an incorrect link to these release notes.

  Workaround: If you made here, then you already know.

  A future release will address this issue.

Release Note Details for Deep Learning Base AMI (Ubuntu) Version 1.0

AWS Deep Learning AMI

The Deep Learning Base AMI are prebuilt with CUDA 8 and 9 and ready for your custom deep learning setup. The Deep Learning Base AMI uses the Anaconda Platform with both Python2 and Python3.

Highlights of the Release

1. Used Ubuntu 2017.09 (ami-8c1be5f6) as the base AMI
2. CUDA 9
3. CuDNN 7
4. NCCL 2.0.5
5. CuBLAS 8 and 9
6. glibc 2.18
7. OpenCV 3.2.0

Python 2.7 and Python 3.5 Support

Python 2.7 and Python 3.6 are supported in the AMI.

CPU Instance Type Support

The AMI supports CPU Instance Types.

GPU Drivers Installed

- Nvidia 384.81
- CUDA 9
- CuDNN 7

Launching Deep Learning Instance

Choose the flavor of the AMI from the list below in the region of your choice and follow the steps at:
AWS Deep Learning AMI Developer Guide

Deep Learning AMI (Ubuntu)

This AMI is available in the following regions:
- US East (Ohio): ec2-us-east-2
- US East (N. Virginia): ec2-us-east-1

- US West (N. California): ec2-us-west-1

- US West (Oregon): ec2-us-west-2

- Asia Pacific (Seoul): ec2-ap-northeast-2

- Asia Pacific (Singapore): ec2-ap-southeast-1

- Asia Pacific (Tokyo): ec2-ap-northeast-1

- EU (Ireland): ec2-eu-west-1

Test Environments

- Built on p2.16xlarge.

- Also tested on p2.xlarge, c4.4xlarge.

Deep Learning Base AMI (Ubuntu) Known Issues

- **Issue**: The MOTD has an incorrect link to these release notes.

  Workaround: If you made here, then you already know.

  A future release will address this issue.

AWS Deep Learning AMI Conda Release Archive

- Release Note Details for Deep Learning AMI (Amazon Linux) Version 2.0
- Release Note Details for Deep Learning AMI (Ubuntu) Version 2.0
- Release Note Details for Deep Learning AMI (Amazon Linux) Version 1.0
- Release Note Details for Deep Learning AMI (Ubuntu) Version 1.0

Release Note Details for Deep Learning AMI (Amazon Linux) Version 2.0

AWS Deep Learning AMI

The AWS Deep Learning AMI are prebuilt with CUDA 8 and 9, and several deep learning frameworks. The DLAMI uses the Anaconda Platform with both Python2 and Python3 to easily switch between frameworks.

Highlights of the Release

1. Used Deep Learning Base AMI (Amazon Linux) as the base AMI
2. CUDA 9
3. CuDNN 7.0.3
4. NCCL 2.1
5. CuBLAS 8 and 9
6. glibc 2.18
7. OpenCV 3.2.0
8. Improved performance of loading Conda environments

Prebuilt Deep Learning Frameworks

- Apache MXNet: MXNet is a flexible, efficient, portable and scalable open source library for deep learning. It supports declarative and imperative programming models, across a wide variety of programming languages, making it powerful yet simple to code deep learning applications. MXNet is efficient, inherently supporting automatic parallel scheduling of portions of source code that can be parallelized over a distributed environment. MXNet is also portable, using memory optimizations that allow it to run on mobile phones to full servers.
  - branch/tag used: v1.0
  - Justification: Stable and well tested
  - To activate:
    - For Anaconda Python2.7+ - `source activate mxnet_p27`
    - For Anaconda Python3+ - `source activate mxnet_p36`
- Caffe2: Caffe2 is a cross-platform framework made with expression, speed, and modularity in mind.
  - branch/tag used: v0.8.1
  - Justification: Stable and well tested
  - Note: Available for Python2.7 only
  - To activate:
    - For Anaconda Python2.7+ - `source activate caffe2_p27`
- CNTK: CNTK - Microsoft Cognitive Toolkit - is a unified deep-learning toolkit by Microsoft Research.
  - branch/tag used : v2.2
  - Justification : Latest release

- To activate:
  - For Anaconda Python2.7+ - `source activate cntk_p27`
  - For Anaconda Python3+ - `source activate cntk_p36`
- Keras: Keras - Deep Learning Library for Python)

Tensorflow integration with v2.0.9

- Justification : Stable release
- To activate:
  - For Anaconda Python2.7+ - `source activate tensorflow_p27`
  - For Anaconda Python3+ - `source activate tensorflow_p36`

MXNet integration with v1.2.2

- Justification : Stable release
- To activate:
  - For Anaconda Python2.7+ - `source activate mxnet_p27`
  - For Anaconda Python3+ - `source activate mxnet_p36`
- PyTorch: PyTorch is a python package that provides two high-level features: Tensor computation (like numpy) with strong GPU acceleration, and Deep Neural Networks built on a tape-based autograd system
  - branch/tag used : v0.3.0
  - Justification : Stable and well tested
  - To activate:
    - For Anaconda Python2.7+ - `source activate pytorch_p27`
    - For Anaconda Python3+ - `source activate pytorch_p36`
- TensorFlow: TensorFlow™ is an open source software library for numerical computation using data flow graphs.
  - branch/tag used : v1.4
  - Justification : Stable and well tested
  - To activate:
    - For Anaconda Python2.7+ - `source activate tensorflow_p27`
    - For Anaconda Python3+ - `source activate tensorflow_p36`
- Theano: Theano is a Python library that allows you to define, optimize, and evaluate mathematical expressions involving multi-dimensional arrays efficiently.
  - branch/tag used: v0.9
  - Justification: Stable and well tested
  - To activate:
    - For Anaconda Python2.7+ - `source activate theano_p27`
    - For Anaconda Python3+ - `source activate theano_p36`

Python 2.7 and Python 3.5 Support

Python 2.7 and Python 3.6 are supported in the AMI for all of this installed Deep Learning Frameworks except Caffe2:

1. Apache MXNet
2. Caffe2 (Python 2.7 only)
3. CNTK
4. Keras
5. PyTorch
6. Tensorflow
7. Theano

CPU Instance Type Support

The AMI supports CPU Instance Types for all frameworks.

GPU Drivers Installed

- CuDNN 7
- Nvidia 384.81
- CUDA 9.0

Launching Deep Learning Instance

Choose the flavor of the AMI from the list below in the region of your choice and follow the steps at:

AWS Deep Learning AMI Developer Guide

Testing the Frameworks

The deep learning frameworks have been tested with MNIST data. The AMI contains scripts to train and test with MNIST for each of the frameworks.

The scripts are available in the /home/ec2-user/src/bin directory.

Deep Learning AMI (Amazon Linux) Regions

Available in the following regions:

Region	Code
US East (Ohio)	ec2-us-east-2
US East (N. Virginia)	ec2-us-east-1
US West (N. California)	ec2-us-west-1
US West (Oregon)	ec2-us-west-2
Beijing (China)	cn-north-1
Asia Pacific (Mumbai)	ec2-ap-south-1

Region	Code
Asia Pacific (Seoul)	ec2-ap-northeast-2
Asia Pacific (Singapore)	ec2-ap-southeast-1
Asia Pacific (Sydney)	ec2-ap-southeast-2
Asia Pacific (Tokyo)	ec2-ap-northeast-1
Canada (Central)	ec2-ca-central-1
EU (Frankfurt)	ec2-eu-central-1
EU (Ireland)	ec2-eu-west-1
EU (London)	ec2-eu-west-2
EU (Paris)	ec2-eu-west-3
SA (Sao Paulo)	ec2-sa-east-1

References

- Apache MXNet
- Caffe2
- CNTK
- Keras
- PyTorch
- TensorFlow
- Theano

Test Environments

- Built on p2.16xlarge.
- Also tested on p2.xlarge, c4.4xlarge.

Known Issues

- **Issue**: PyTorch tests are broken. ~/src/bin/testPyTorch - installs test environment that is not compatible with the pytorch 0.3.0

  Workaround: N/A

- **Issue**: Tutorials provided by the framework or third parties may have Python dependencies not installed on the DLAMI.

  Workaround: You will need to install those while in the activated environment with conda or pip.

- **Issue**: Module not found error running Caffe2 examples.

  Workaround: Caffe2 optional dependencies are needed for some tutorials

- **Issue**: Caffe2 model download features result in 404. The models have changed locations since the v0.8.1 release. Update models/download.py to use the update from master.

- **Issue**: matplotlib can only render png.

  Workaround: Install Pillow then restart your kernel.

- **Issue**: Changing Caffe2 source code doesn't seem to work.

  Workaround: Change your PYTHONPATH to use the install location `/usr/local/caffe2` instead of the build folder.

- **Issue**: Caffe2 net_drawer errors.

  Workaround: Use the logger patch found in this commit.

- **Issue**: Caffe2 example shows an error regarding LMDB (can't open DB, etc.)

  Workaround: This will require a build from source after installing system LMDB, such as: `sudo apt-get install liblmdb-dev`

- **Issue**: SSH disconnects while using Jupyter server ties up your local port. When trying create a tunnel to the server you see `channel_setup_fwd_listener_tcpip: cannot listen to port: 8057`.

  Workaround: Use `lsof -ti:8057 | xargs kill -9` where 8057 is the local port you used. Then try to create the tunnel to your Jupyter server again.

Release Note Details for Deep Learning AMI (Ubuntu) Version 2.0

AWS Deep Learning AMI

The AWS Deep Learning AMI are prebuilt with CUDA 8 and 9, and several deep learning frameworks. The DLAMI uses the Anaconda Platform with both Python2 and Python3 to easily switch between frameworks.

Highlights of the Release

1. Used Deep Learning Base AMI (Ubuntu) as the base AMI
2. CUDA 9
3. CuDNN 7
4. NCCL 2.1
5. CuBLAS 8 and 9
6. glibc 2.18
7. OpenCV 3.2.0
8. Improved performance of loading Conda environments

Pre-built Deep Learning Frameworks

- Apache MXNet: MXNet is a flexible, efficient, portable and scalable open source library for deep learning. It supports declarative and imperative programming models, across a wide variety of programming languages, making it powerful yet simple to code deep learning applications. MXNet is efficient, inherently supporting automatic parallel scheduling of portions of source code that can be parallelized over a distributed environment. MXNet is also portable, using memory optimizations that allow it to run on mobile phones to full servers.
    - branch/tag used: v1.0
    - Justification: Stable and well tested
    - To activate:
        - For Anaconda Python2.7+ - `source activate mxnet_p27`
        - For Anaconda Python3+ - `source activate mxnet_p36`
- Caffe2: Caffe2 is a cross-platform framework made with expression, speed, and modularity in mind.
    - branch/tag used: v0.8.1
    - Justification: Stable and well tested
    - Note: Available for Python2.7 only
    - To activate:
        - For Anaconda Python2.7+ - `source activate caffe2_p27`
- CNTK: CNTK - Microsoft Cognitive Toolkit - is a unified deep-learning toolkit by Microsoft Research.
    - branch/tag used : v2.2
    - Justification : Latest release
    - To activate:

- For Anaconda Python2.7+ - `source activate cntk_p27`
- For Anaconda Python3+ - `source activate cntk_p36`

- Keras: Keras - Deep Learning Library for Python)

Tensorflow integration with v2.0.9

  - Justification : Stable release
  - To activate:
    - For Anaconda Python2.7+ - `source activate tensorflow_p27`
    - For Anaconda Python3+ - `source activate tensorflow_p36`

MXNet integration with v1.2.2

  - Justification : Stable release
  - To activate:
    - For Anaconda Python2.7+ - `source activate mxnet_p27`
    - For Anaconda Python3+ - `source activate mxnet_p36`

- PyTorch: PyTorch is a python package that provides two high-level features: Tensor computation (like numpy) with strong GPU acceleration, and Deep Neural Networks built on a tape-based autograd system
  - branch/tag used : v0.3.0
  - Justification : Stable and well tested
  - To activate:
    - For Anaconda Python2.7+ - `source activate pytorch_p27`
    - For Anaconda Python3+ - `source activate pytorch_p36`

- TensorFlow: TensorFlow™ is an open source software library for numerical computation using data flow graphs.
  - branch/tag used : v1.4
  - Justification : Stable and well tested
  - To activate:
    - For Anaconda Python2.7+ - `source activate tensorflow_p27`
    - For Anaconda Python3+ - `source activate tensorflow_p36`

- Theano: Theano is a Python library that allows you to define, optimize, and evaluate mathematical expressions involving multi-dimensional arrays efficiently.
  - branch/tag used: v0.9
  - Justification: Stable and well tested
  - To activate:
    - For Anaconda Python2.7+ - `source activate theano_p27`
    - For Anaconda Python3+ - `source activate theano_p36`

Python 2.7 and Python 3.5 Support

Python 2.7 and Python 3.6 are supported in the AMI for all of this installed Deep Learning Frameworks except Caffe2:

1. Apache MXNet
2. Caffe2 (Python 2.7 only)
3. CNTK
4. Keras
5. PyTorch
6. Tensorflow
7. Theano

CPU Instance Type Support

The AMI supports CPU Instance Types for all frameworks. MXNet is built with support for Intel MKL2017 DNN library support.

GPU Drivers Installed

- CuDNN 7
- NVIDIA 384.81
- CUDA 9.0

Launching Deep Learning Instance

Choose the flavor of the AMI from the list below in the region of your choice and follow the steps at:

AWS Deep Learning AMI Developer Guide

Testing the Frameworks

The deep learning frameworks have been tested with MNIST data. The AMI contains scripts to train and test with MNIST for each of the frameworks.

The scripts are available in the /home/ubuntu/src/bin directory.

Deep Learning AMI (Ubuntu) Regions

Available in the following regions:

Region	Code
US East (Ohio)	ec2-us-east-2
US East (N. Virginia)	ec2-us-east-1
US West (N. California)	ec2-us-west-1
US West (Oregon)	ec2-us-west-2
Beijing (China)	cn-north-1

Region	Code
Asia Pacific (Mumbai)	ec2-ap-south-1
Asia Pacific (Seoul)	ec2-ap-northeast-2
Asia Pacific (Singapore)	ec2-ap-southeast-1
Asia Pacific (Sydney)	ec2-ap-southeast-2
Asia Pacific (Tokyo)	ec2-ap-northeast-1
Canada (Central)	ec2-ca-central-1
EU (Frankfurt)	ec2-eu-central-1
EU (Ireland)	ec2-eu-west-1
EU (London)	ec2-eu-west-2
EU (Paris)	ec2-eu-west-3
SA (Sao Paulo)	ec2-sa-east-1

References

- Apache MXNet
- Caffe2
- CNTK
- Keras
- PyTorch
- TensorFlow
- Theano

Test Environments

- Built on p2.16xlarge.
- Also tested on p2.xlarge, c4.4xlarge.

Known Issues

- **Issue:** PyTorch tests are broken. ~/src/bin/testPyTorch - installs test environment that is not compatible with the pytorch 0.3.0

  Workaround: N/A

- **Issue:** Tutorials provided by the framework or third parties may have Python dependencies not installed on the DLAMI.

  Workaround: You will need to install those while in the activated environment with conda or pip.

- **Issue:** Module not found error running Caffe2 examples.

  Workaround: Caffe2 optional dependencies are needed for some tutorials

- **Issue:** Caffe2 model download features result in 404. The models have changed locations since the v0.8.1 release. Update models/download.py to use the update from master.

- **Issue:** matplotlib can only render png.

  Workaround: Install Pillow then restart your kernel.

- **Issue**: Changing Caffe2 source code doesn't seem to work.

  Workaround: Change your PYTHONPATH to use the install location `/usr/local/caffe2` instead of the build folder.

- **Issue**: Caffe2 net_drawer errors.

  Workaround: Use the logger patch found in this commit.

- **Issue**: Caffe2 example shows an error regarding LMDB (can't open DB, etc.)

  Workaround: This will require a build from source after installing system LMDB, such as: `sudo apt-get install liblmdb-dev`

- **Issue**: SSH disconnects while using Jupyter server ties up your local port. When trying create a tunnel to the server you see `channel_setup_fwd_listener_tcpip: cannot listen to port: 8057`.

  Workaround: Use `lsof -ti:8057 | xargs kill -9` where 8057 is the local port you used. Then try to create the tunnel to your Jupyter server again.

Release Note Details for Deep Learning AMI (Amazon Linux) Version 1.0

AWS Deep Learning AMI

The AWS Deep Learning AMI are prebuilt with CUDA 8 and 9, and several deep learning frameworks. The DLAMI uses the Anaconda Platform with both Python2 and Python3 to easily switch between frameworks.

Highlights of the Release

1. Used Amazon Linux 2017.09 (ami-8c1be5f6) as the base AMI
2. CUDA 9
3. CuDNN 7.0.3
4. NCCL 2.0.5
5. CuBLAS 8 and 9
6. glibc 2.18
7. OpenCV 3.2.0

Prebuilt Deep Learning Frameworks

- Apache MXNet: MXNet is a flexible, efficient, portable and scalable open source library for deep learning. It supports declarative and imperative programming models, across a wide variety of programming languages, making it powerful yet simple to code deep learning applications. MXNet is efficient, inherently supporting automatic parallel scheduling of portions of source code that can be parallelized over a distributed environment. MXNet is also portable, using memory optimizations that allow it to run on mobile phones to full servers.
  - branch/tag used: v0.12.0
  - Justification: Stable and well tested
  - To activate:
    - For Anaconda Python2.7+ - `source activate mxnet_p27`
    - For Anaconda Python3+ - `source activate mxnet_p36`
- Caffe2: Caffe2 is a cross-platform framework made with expression, speed, and modularity in mind.
  - branch/tag used: v0.8.1
  - Justification: Stable and well tested
  - Note: Available for Python2.7 only
  - To activate:
    - For Anaconda Python2.7+ - `source activate caffe2_p27`
- CNTK: CNTK - Microsoft Cognitive Toolkit - is a unified deep-learning toolkit by Microsoft Research.
  - branch/tag used : v2.2
  - Justification : Latest release
  - To activate:

- For Anaconda Python2.7+ - `source activate cntk_p27`
- For Anaconda Python3+ - `source activate cntk_p36`

- Keras: Keras - Deep Learning Library for Python)

  Tensorflow integration with v2.0.9

  - Justification : Stable release
  - To activate:
    - For Anaconda Python2.7+ - `source activate tensorflow_p27`
    - For Anaconda Python3+ - `source activate tensorflow_p36`

  MXNet integration with v1.2.2

  - Justification : Stable release
  - To activate:
    - For Anaconda Python2.7+ - `source activate mxnet_p27`
    - For Anaconda Python3+ - `source activate mxnet_p36`

- PyTorch: PyTorch is a python package that provides two high-level features: Tensor computation (like numpy) with strong GPU acceleration, and Deep Neural Networks built on a tape-based autograd system

  - branch/tag used : v0.2
  - Justification : Stable and well tested
  - To activate:
    - For Anaconda Python2.7+ - `source activate pytorch_p27`
    - For Anaconda Python3+ - `source activate pytorch_p36`

- TensorFlow: TensorFlow™ is an open source software library for numerical computation using data flow graphs.

  - branch/tag used : v1.4
  - Justification : Stable and well tested
  - To activate:
    - For Anaconda Python2.7+ - `source activate tensorflow_p27`
    - For Anaconda Python3+ - `source activate tensorflow_p36`

- Theano: Theano is a Python library that allows you to define, optimize, and evaluate mathematical expressions involving multi-dimensional arrays efficiently.

  - branch/tag used: v0.9
  - Justification: Stable and well tested
  - To activate:
    - For Anaconda Python2.7+ - `source activate theano_p27`
    - For Anaconda Python3+ - `source activate theano_p36`

Python 2.7 and Python 3.5 Support

Python 2.7 and Python 3.6 are supported in the AMI for all of this installed Deep Learning Frameworks except Caffe2:

1. Apache MXNet
2. Caffe2 (Python 2.7 only)
3. CNTK
4. PyTorch
5. Tensorflow
6. Theano

CPU Instance Type Support

The AMI supports CPU Instance Types for all frameworks.

GPU Drivers Installed

- CuDNN 7
- Nvidia 384.81
- CUDA 9.0

Launching Deep Learning Instance

Choose the flavor of the AMI from the list below in the region of your choice and follow the steps at:

AWS Deep Learning AMI Developer Guide

Testing the Frameworks

The deep learning frameworks have been tested with MNIST data. The AMI contains scripts to train and test with MNIST for each of the frameworks.

The scripts are available in the /home/ec2-user/src/bin directory.

Deep Learning AMI (Amazon Linux) Regions

Deep Learning AMI (Amazon Linux)s are available in the following regions:

- US East (Ohio): ec2-us-east-2
- US East (N. Virginia): ec2-us-east-1
- US West (N. California): ec2-us-west-1
- US West (Oregon): ec2-us-west-2
- Asia Pacific (Seoul): ec2-ap-northeast-2
- Asia Pacific (Singapore): ec2-ap-southeast-1
- Asia Pacific (Tokyo): ec2-ap-northeast-1

- EU (Ireland): ec2-eu-west-1

References

- Apache MXNet
- Caffe2
- CNTK
- Keras
- PyTorch
- TensorFlow
- Theano

Test Environments

- Built on p2.16xlarge.
- Also tested on p2.xlarge, c4.4xlarge.

Deep Learning AMI (Amazon Linux) Known Issues

- **Issue**: Versions of pip and Python are not compatible for the Amazon Linux Deep Learning AMI (DLAMI), specifically pip, which is expected to install Python 2 bindings, but instead installs Python 3 bindings.

  This is a known problem documented on the pip website. A future release will address this issue.

  Workaround: Use the relevant command below to install the package for the appropriate Python version:

  python2.7 -m pip install *some-python-package*

  python3.4 -m pip install *some-python-package*

- **Issue**: Tutorials provided by the framework or third parties may have Python dependencies not installed on the DLAMI.

  Workaround: You will need to install those while in the activated environment with conda or pip.

- **Issue**: Module not found error running Caffe2 examples.

  Workaround: Caffe2 optional dependencies are needed for some tutorials

- **Issue**: Caffe2 model download features result in 404. The models have changed locations since the v0.8.1 release. Update models/download.py to use the update from master.

- **Issue**: matplotlib can only render png.

  Workaround: Install Pillow then restart your kernel.

- **Issue**: Changing Caffe2 source code doesn't seem to work.

  Workaround: Change your PYTHONPATH to use the install location `/usr/local/caffe2` instead of the build folder.

- **Issue**: Caffe2 net_drawer errors.

  Workaround: Use the logger patch found in this commit.

112

- **Issue**: Caffe2 example shows an error regarding LMDB (can't open DB, etc.)

  Workaround: This will require a build from source after installing system LMDB, such as: `sudo apt-get install liblmdb-dev`

- **Issue**: SSH disconnects while using Jupyter server ties up your local port. When trying create a tunnel to the server you see `channel_setup_fwd_listener_tcpip: cannot listen to port: 8157`.

  Workaround: Use `lsof -ti:8057 | xargs kill -9` where 8057 is the local port you used. Then try to create the tunnel to your Jupyter server again.

  Issue: The MOTD has an incorrect link to these release notes.

  Workaround: If you made here, then you already know.

  A future release will address this issue.

Release Note Details for Deep Learning AMI (Ubuntu) Version 1.0

AWS Deep Learning AMI

The AWS Deep Learning AMI are prebuilt with CUDA 8 and 9, and several deep learning frameworks. The DLAMI uses the Anaconda Platform with both Python2 and Python3 to easily switch between frameworks.

Highlights of the Release

1. Used Ubuntu 2017.09 (ami-8c1be5f6) as the base AMI
2. CUDA 9
3. CuDNN 7
4. NCCL 2.0.5
5. CuBLAS 8 and 9
6. glibc 2.18
7. OpenCV 3.2.0

Pre-built Deep Learning Frameworks

- Apache MXNet: MXNet is a flexible, efficient, portable and scalable open source library for deep learning. It supports declarative and imperative programming models, across a wide variety of programming languages, making it powerful yet simple to code deep learning applications. MXNet is efficient, inherently supporting automatic parallel scheduling of portions of source code that can be parallelized over a distributed environment. MXNet is also portable, using memory optimizations that allow it to run on mobile phones to full servers.
    - branch/tag used: v0.12.0
    - Justification: Stable and well tested
    - To activate:
        - For Anaconda Python2.7+ - `source activate mxnet_p27`
        - For Anaconda Python3+ - `source activate mxnet_p36`
- Caffe2: Caffe2 is a cross-platform framework made with expression, speed, and modularity in mind.
    - branch/tag used: v0.8.1
    - Justification: Stable and well tested
    - Note: Available for Python2.7 only
    - To activate:
        - For Anaconda Python2.7+ - `source activate caffe2_p27`
- CNTK: CNTK - Microsoft Cognitive Toolkit - is a unified deep-learning toolkit by Microsoft Research.
    - branch/tag used : v2.2
    - Justification : Latest release
    - To activate:
        - For Anaconda Python2.7+ - `source activate cntk_p27`

- For Anaconda Python3+ - `source activate cntk_p36`
- Keras: Keras - Deep Learning Library for Python)

Tensorflow integration with v2.0.9

  - Justification : Stable release
  - To activate:
    - For Anaconda Python2.7+ - `source activate tensorflow_p27`
    - For Anaconda Python3+ - `source activate tensorflow_p36`

MXNet integration with v1.2.2

  - Justification : Stable release
  - To activate:
    - For Anaconda Python2.7+ - `source activate mxnet_p27`
    - For Anaconda Python3+ - `source activate mxnet_p36`

- PyTorch: PyTorch is a python package that provides two high-level features: Tensor computation (like numpy) with strong GPU acceleration, and Deep Neural Networks built on a tape-based autograd system

  - branch/tag used : v0.2
  - Justification : Stable and well tested
  - To activate:
    - For Anaconda Python2.7+ - `source activate pytorch_p27`
    - For Anaconda Python3+ - `source activate pytorch_p36`

- TensorFlow: TensorFlow™ is an open source software library for numerical computation using data flow graphs.

  - branch/tag used : v1.4
  - Justification : Stable and well tested
  - To activate:
    - For Anaconda Python2.7+ - `source activate tensorflow_p27`
    - For Anaconda Python3+ - `source activate tensorflow_p36`

- Theano: Theano is a Python library that allows you to define, optimize, and evaluate mathematical expressions involving multi-dimensional arrays efficiently.

  - branch/tag used: v0.9
  - Justification: Stable and well tested
  - To activate:
    - For Anaconda Python2.7+ - `source activate theano_p27`
    - For Anaconda Python3+ - `source activate theano_p36`

Python 2.7 and Python 3.5 Support

Python 2.7 and Python 3.6 are supported in the AMI for all of this installed Deep Learning Frameworks except Caffe2:

1. Apache MXNet

2. Caffe2 (Python 2.7 only)

3. CNTK

4. PyTorch

5. Tensorflow

6. Theano

CPU Instance Type Support

The AMI supports CPU Instance Types for all frameworks. MXNet is built with support for Intel MKL2017 DNN library support.

GPU Drivers Installed

- CuDNN 7
- NVIDIA 384.81
- CUDA 9.0

Launching Deep Learning Instance

Choose the flavor of the AMI from the list below in the region of your choice and follow the steps at:

AWS Deep Learning AMI Developer Guide

Testing the Frameworks

The deep learning frameworks have been tested with MNIST data. The AMI contains scripts to train and test with MNIST for each of the frameworks.

The scripts are available in the /home/ubuntu/src/bin directory.

Deep Learning AMI (Ubuntu) Regions

Deep Learning AMI (Ubuntu)s are available in the following regions:

- US East (Ohio): ec2-us-east-2
- US East (N. Virginia): ec2-us-east-1
- US West (N. California): ec2-us-west-1
- US West (Oregon): ec2-us-west-2
- Asia Pacific (Seoul): ec2-ap-northeast-2
- Asia Pacific (Singapore): ec2-ap-southeast-1
- Asia Pacific (Tokyo): ec2-ap-northeast-1
- EU (Ireland): ec2-eu-west-1

References

- Apache MXNet
- Caffe2
- CNTK
- Keras
- PyTorch
- TensorFlow
- Theano

Test Environments

- Built on p2.16xlarge.
- Also tested on p2.xlarge, c4.4xlarge.

Deep Learning AMI (Ubuntu) Known Issues

- **Issue**: Tutorials provided by the framework or third parties may have Python dependencies not installed on the DLAMI.

  Workaround: You will need to install those while in the activated environment with conda or pip.

- **Issue**: Module not found error running Caffe2 examples.

  Workaround: Caffe2 optional dependencies are needed for some tutorials

- **Issue**: Caffe2 model download features result in 404. The models have changed locations since the v0.8.1 release. Update models/download.py to use the update from master.

- **Issue**: matplotlib can only render png.

  Workaround: Install Pillow then restart your kernel.

- **Issue**: Changing Caffe2 source code doesn't seem to work.

  Workaround: Change your PYTHONPATH to use the install location `/usr/local/caffe2` instead of the build folder.

- **Issue**: Caffe2 net_drawer errors.

  Workaround: Use the logger patch found in this commit.

- **Issue**: Caffe2 example shows an error regarding LMDB (can't open DB, etc.)

  Workaround: This will require a build from source after installing system LMDB, such as: `sudo apt-get install liblmdb-dev`

- **Issue**: SSH disconnects while using Jupyter server ties up your local port. When trying create a tunnel to the server you see `channel_setup_fwd_listener_tcpip: cannot listen to port: 8157`.

  Workaround: Use `lsof -ti:8057 | xargs kill -9` where 8057 is the local port you used. Then try to create the tunnel to your Jupyter server again.

  Problem: The MOTD has an incorrect link to these release notes.

  Workaround: If you made here, then you already know.

  A future release will address this issue.

AWS Deep Learning AMI Source Release Archive

- Deep Learning AMI with Source Code (CUDA 9, Ubuntu) Version: 2.0
- Deep Learning AMI Ubuntu Version: 2.4_Oct2017
- Ubuntu DLAMI Release Archive
- Amazon Linux DLAMI Release Archive

Deep Learning AMI with Source Code (CUDA 9, Ubuntu) Version: 2.0

Deep Learning Amazon Machine Image

The Deep Learning AMIs are prebuilt with CUDA9 and MXNet and also contain the Anaconda Platform (Python2 and Python3).

Highlights of the Release

1. Used Deep Learning Base AMI (Ubuntu) as the base AMI

2. Refreshed TensorFlow master with CUDA9/Volta support

3. MXNet upgraded to v1.0

4. Upgraded PyTorch to v0.3.0

5. Added Keras 2.0.9 support with TensorFlow as the default backend

Prebuilt Deep Learning Frameworks

- Apache MXNet: MXNet is a flexible, efficient, portable and scalable open source library for deep learning. It supports declarative and imperative programming models, across a wide variety of programming languages, making it powerful yet simple to code deep learning applications. MXNet is efficient, inherently supporting automatic parallel scheduling of portions of source code that can be parallelized over a distributed environment. MXNet is also portable, using memory optimizations that allow it to run on mobile phones to full servers.
    - branch/tag used: v1.0
    - Justification: Stable and well tested
    - Source Directories:
        - /home/ubuntu/src/mxnet
- Caffe2: Caffe2 is a cross-platform framework made with expression, speed, and modularity in mind.
    - branch/tag used: v0.8.1 tag
    - Justification: Stable and well tested
    - Note: Available for Python2.7 only
    - Source Directories:
        - For Python2.7+ - /home/ec2-user/src/caffe2
        - For Anaconda Python2.7+ - /home/ec2-user/src/caffe2_anaconda2
- Keras: Keras - Deep Learning Library for Python)

    Tensorflow integration with v2.0.9. Tensorflow is the default backend.
    - Justification : Stable release
    - Source Directories:
        - /home/ec2-user/src/keras

- PyTorch: PyTorch is a python package that provides two high-level features: Tensor computation (like numpy) with strong GPU acceleration, and Deep Neural Networks built on a tape-based autograd system.
  - branch/tag used: v0.3.0
  - Justification: Stable and well tested
  - Source_Directories:
    - /home/ubuntu/src/pytorch
- TensorFlow: TensorFlow™ is an open source software library for numerical computation using data flow graphs.
  - branch/tag used : Master tag
  - Justification : Stable and well tested
  - Source Directories :
    - For Python2.7+ - /home/ubuntu/src/caffe
    - For Python3+ - /home/ubuntu/src/caffe3
    - For Anaconda Python2.7+ - /home/ubuntu/src/caffe_anaconda2
    - For Anaconda3 Python3+ - /home/ubuntu/src/caffe_anaconda3
    - For CPU_ONLY : /home/ubuntu/src/caffe_cpu

Python 2.7 and Python 3.5 Support

Python 2.7 and Python 3.5 are supported in the AMI for the following Deep Learning Frameworks:

1. Apache MXNet
2. Caffe2
3. Keras
4. PyTorch
5. Tensorflow

CPU Instance Type Support

The AMI supports CPU Instance Types for all frameworks. MXNet is built with support for Intel MKL2017 DNN library support.

GPU Drivers Installed

- CuDNN 7
- Nvidia 384.81
- CUDA 9.0

Launching Deep Learning Instance

Choose the flavor of the AMI from the list below in the region of your choice and follow the steps at:

EC2 Documentation to launch P2 Instance

Testing the FrameWorks

The Deep Learning frameworks have been tested with MNIST data. The AMI contains scripts to train and test with MNIST for each of the frameworks.

The scripts are available in the /home/ubuntu/src/bin directory.

The following scripts test the various frameworks:

/home/ubuntu/src/bin/testMXNet : tests MXNet

/home/ubuntu/src/bin/testTensorFlow : tests TensorFlow

/home/ubuntu/src/bin/testCaffe2 : tests Caffe2

The following tests have been run against each of the frameworks:

- MXNet: This example inside the MXNet repository. Validation accuracy threshold tested for is 97%.
- Tensorflow: This example inside the keras repository. Validation accuracy threshold tested for is 95%.
- Caffe2: Based on this example inside the Caffe2 repository. Validation accuracy threshold is 90%.

AMI Region Availability

Available in the following regions:

Region	Code
US East (Ohio)	ec2-us-east-2
US East (N. Virginia)	ec2-us-east-1
US West (N. California)	ec2-us-west-1
US West (Oregon)	ec2-us-west-2
Beijing (China)	cn-north-1
Asia Pacific (Mumbai)	ec2-ap-south-1
Asia Pacific (Seoul)	ec2-ap-northeast-2
Asia Pacific (Singapore)	ec2-ap-southeast-1
Asia Pacific (Sydney)	ec2-ap-southeast-2
Asia Pacific (Tokyo)	ec2-ap-northeast-1
Canada (Central)	ec2-ca-central-1
EU (Frankfurt)	ec2-eu-central-1
EU (Ireland)	ec2-eu-west-1
EU (London)	ec2-eu-west-2
EU (Paris)	ec2-eu-west-3
SA (Sao Paulo)	ec2-sa-east-1

References

- Apache MXNet
- Caffe2
- CNTK
- Keras
- PyTorch
- TensorFlow

- Theano

Test Environments

- Built on p2.16xlarge.
- Also tested on p2.xlarge, c4.4xlarge.

Known Issues

- **Issue**: NCCL is not fully supported. Attempts to use NCCL with any instances but P3 will lead to a crash.

  Workaround: Do not use NCCL on instances other than P3.

- **Issue**: PyTorch tests are broken. ~/src/bin/testPyTorch - installs test environment that is not compatible with the pytorch 0.3.0

  Workaround: N/A

- **Issue**: Tutorials provided by the framework or third parties may have Python dependencies not installed on the DLAMI.

  Workaround: You will need to install those while in the activated environment with conda or pip.

- **Issue**: Module not found error running Caffe2 examples.

  Workaround: Caffe2 optional dependencies are needed for some tutorials

- **Issue**: Caffe2 model download features result in 404. The models have changed locations since the v0.8.1 release. Update models/download.py to use the update from master.

- **Issue**: matplotlib can only render png.

  Workaround: Install Pillow then restart your kernel.

- **Issue**: Changing Caffe2 source code doesn't seem to work.

  Workaround: Change your PYTHONPATH to use the install location `/usr/local/caffe2` instead of the build folder.

- **Issue**: Caffe2 net_drawer errors.

  Workaround: Use the logger patch found in this commit.

- **Issue**: Caffe2 example shows an error regarding LMDB (can't open DB, etc.)

  Workaround: This will require a build from source after installing system LMDB, such as: `sudo apt-get install liblmdb-dev`

- **Issue**: SSH disconnects while using Jupyter server ties up your local port. When trying create a tunnel to the server you see `channel_setup_fwd_listener_tcpip: cannot listen to port: 8057`.

  Workaround: Use `lsof -ti:8057 | xargs kill -9` where 8057 is the local port you used. Then try to create the tunnel to your Jupyter server again.

Deep Learning AMI Ubuntu Version: 2.4_Oct2017

Deep Learning Amazon Machine Image

The Deep Learning AMIs are pre-built with popular Deep Learning frameworks and also contain the Anaconda Platform (Python2 and Python3).

Highlights of the Release

1. Used Ubuntu 16.04 (ami-d15a75c7) as the base AMI

2. CUDA 8 support

3. Framework upgrades for Tensorflow(v1.3.0), Caffe2(v0.8.0), Caffe(1.0), CNTK(v2.0), Theano(rel-0.9.0)

Pre-built Deep Learning Frameworks

- MXNet: MXNet is a flexible, efficient, portable and scalable open source library for deep learning. It supports declarative and imperative programming models, across a wide variety of programming languages, making it powerful yet simple to code deep learning applications. MXNet is efficient, inherently supporting automatic parallel scheduling of portions of source code that can be parallelized over a distributed environment. MXNet is also portable, using memory optimizations that allow it to run on mobile phones to full servers.

  - branch/tag used: v0.11.0 tag

  - Justification: Stable and well tested

  - Source_Directories:

    - /home/ubuntu/src/mxnet

- Caffe: Caffe is a deep learning framework made with expression, speed, and modularity in mind. It is developed by the Berkeley Vision and Learning Center (BVLC) and by community contributors.

  - branch/tag used: v1.0 tag

  - Justification: Supports cuda8.0 and cudnn 5.1

  - Source_Directories:

    - For Python2.7+ - /home/ubuntu/src/caffe

    - For Python3+ - /home/ubuntu/src/caffe3

    - For Anaconda Python2.7+ - /home/ubuntu/src/caffe_anaconda2

    - For Anaconda3 Python3+ - /home/ubuntu/src/caffe_anaconda3

    - For CPU_ONLY : /home/ubuntu/src/caffe_cpu

- Caffe2: Caffe2 is a cross-platform framework made with expression, speed, and modularity in mind.

  - branch/tag used: v0.8.0 tag

  - Justification: Stable and well tested

  - Note: This is an experimental release and there may be some issues. Available for Python2.7 only

  - Source_Directories:

    - For Python2.7+ - /home/ubuntu/src/caffe2

123

- For Anaconda Python2.7+ - /home/ubuntu/src/caffe2_anaconda2
- Theano: Theano is a Python library that allows you to define, optimize, and evaluate mathematical expressions involving multi-dimensional arrays efficiently.
  - branch/tag used: rel-0.9.0 tag
  - Justification: Stable and well tested
  - Source_Directories:
    - /home/ubuntu/src/Theano
- TensorFlow: TensorFlow™ is an open source software library for numerical computation using data flow graphs.
  - branch/tag used : v1.3.0 tag
  - Justification : Stable and well tested
  - Source_Directories :
    - For Python2.7+ - /home/ubuntu/src/tensorflow
    - For Python3+ - /home/ubuntu/src/tensorflow3
    - For Anaconda Python2.7+ - /home/ubuntu/src/tensorflow_anaconda
    - For Anaconda Python3+ - /home/ubuntu/src/tensorflow_anaconda3
- Torch: Torch is a scientific computing framework with wide support for machine learning algorithms that puts GPUs first. It is easy to use and efficient, thanks to an easy and fast scripting language, LuaJIT, and an underlying C/CUDA implementation.
  - branch/tag used : master branch
  - Justification : No other stable branch or tag available
  - Source_Directories :
    - /home/ubuntu/src/torch
- CNTK: CNTK - Microsoft Cognitive Toolkit - is a unified deep-learning toolkit by Microsoft Research.
  - branch/tag used : v2.0 tag
  - Justification : Stable release
  - Source_Directories :
    - /home/ubuntu/src/cntk
- Keras: Keras - Deep Learning Library for Python)
  - branch/tag used : v2.0.8
  - Justification : Stable release
  - Source_Directories:
    - /home/ubuntu/src/keras

Python 2.7 and Python 3.5 Support

Python 2.7 and Python 3.5 are supported in the AMI for the following Deep Learning Frameworks:

1. Caffe
2. Tensorflow

3. Theano

4. MXNet

5. CNTK

CPU Instance Type Support

The AMI supports CPU Instance Types for all frameworks. MXNet is built with support for Intel MKL2017 DNN library support. If you want to use the caffe binary for the CPU instance, then you should use the binary inside /home/ubuntu/src/caffe_cpu/

CNTK Python Support

You can run CNTK for Python inside a conda environment. To do this:

```
1  cd /home/ubuntu/src/anaconda3/bin
2  source activate cntk-py34
```

GPU Drivers Installed

- CuDNN 5.1

- NVIDIA 375.66

- CUDA 8.0

Launching Deep Learning Instance

Choose the flavor of the AMI from the list below in the region of your choice and follow the steps at:

EC2 Documentation to launch P2 Instance

Testing the Frameworks

The Deep Learning frameworks have been tested with MNIST data. The AMI contains scripts to train and test with MNIST for each of the frameworks. The test checks if the validation accuracy is above a specific threshold. The threshold is different for each of the frameworks.

The scripts are available in the /home/ubuntu/src/bin directory.

The following scripts test the various frameworks:

/home/ubuntu/src/bin/testAll : tests all frameworks

/home/ubuntu/src/bin/testMXNet : tests MXNet

/home/ubuntu/src/bin/testTheano : tests Theano

/home/ubuntu/src/bin/testTensorFlow : tests TensorFlow

/home/ubuntu/src/bin/testTorch : tests Torch

/home/ubuntu/src/bin/testCNTK : tests CNTK

/home/ubuntu/src/bin/testCaffe2 : tests Caffe2

The following tests have been run against each of the frameworks:

- MXNet: This example inside the MXNet repository. Validation accuracy threshold tested for is 97%.

- Tensorflow: This example inside the keras repository. Validation accuracy threshold tested for is 95%.

- Theano: The same example above. Validation accuracy threshold is 95%.

- Torch: This example inside the Torch tree. Validation accuracy threshold is 93%.

- Caffe: This example inside the Caffe repository. Validation accuracy threshold is 98%.

- CNTK: This example inside the CNTK repository. Validation accuracy threshold is 97%.

- Caffe2: Based on this example inside the Caffe2 repository. Validation accuracy threshold is 90%.

Ubuntu AMI

Ubuntu based Deep Learning AMIs are available in the following regions:

Region	Code
US East (Ohio)	ec2-us-east-2
US East (N. Virginia)	ec2-us-east-1
US West (N. California)	ec2-us-west-1
US West (Oregon)	ec2-us-west-2
Beijing (China)	cn-north-1
Asia Pacific (Mumbai)	ec2-ap-south-1
Asia Pacific (Seoul)	ec2-ap-northeast-2
Asia Pacific (Singapore)	ec2-ap-southeast-1
Asia Pacific (Sydney)	ec2-ap-southeast-2
Asia Pacific (Tokyo)	ec2-ap-northeast-1
Canada (Central)	ec2-ca-central-1
EU (Frankfurt)	ec2-eu-central-1
EU (Ireland)	ec2-eu-west-1
EU (London)	ec2-eu-west-2
EU (Paris)	ec2-eu-west-3
SA (Sao Paulo)	ec2-sa-east-1

References

MXNet

Caffe

Theano

TensorFlow

Torch

CNTK

Test Environments

- Built on p2.16xlarge.

- Also tested on p2.xlarge, p2.8xlarge, p2.16xlarge, c4.4xlarge.

Known Issues

- Need to use sudo to run the testCNTK script.

  e.g. sudo ./testCNTK

- The conda environments keras1.2_p3 and keras1.2_p2 come with CPU only version of MXNet.

  To use Keras with an MXNet backend to train on GPUs, you can workaround this issue by running the following:

```
1 pip install mxnet-cu80
```

  from inside the conda environment.

Not Supported

- Functioning of multiple frameworks together in the same Python process has not been tested.

  For example, a code snippet like the following:

```
1 import mxnet as mx
2 import tensorflow as tf
```

  in the same Python process may cause an issue.

Ubuntu DLAMI Release Archive

- Deep Learning CUDA 9 AMI Ubuntu Version: 1.0
- Deep Learning AMI Ubuntu Version: 2.3_Sep2017
- Deep Learning AMI Ubuntu Version: 2.2_August2017
- Deep Learning AMI Ubuntu Version: 1.5_June2017
- Deep Learning AMI Ubuntu Version: 1.4_June2017
- Deep Learning AMI Ubuntu Version: 1.3_Apr2017
- Deep Learning AMI Ubuntu Version: 1.2
- Deep Learning AMI Ubuntu Version: 1.1
- Deep Learning AMI Ubuntu Version: 1.0

Deep Learning CUDA 9 AMI Ubuntu Version: 1.0

Deep Learning Amazon Machine Image

The Deep Learning AMIs are prebuilt with CUDA9 and MXNet and also contain the Anaconda Platform (Python2 and Python3).

Highlights of the Release

1. Used Ubuntu 16.04 (ami-d15a75c7) as the base AMI
2. CUDA 9
3. CuDNN 7
4. NCCL 2.0
5. MXNet with CUDA9 Support

Prebuilt Deep Learning Frameworks

- MXNet: MXNet is a flexible, efficient, portable and scalable open source library for deep learning. It supports declarative and imperative programming models, across a wide variety of programming languages, making it powerful yet simple to code deep learning applications. MXNet is efficient, inherently supporting automatic parallel scheduling of portions of source code that can be parallelized over a distributed environment. MXNet is also portable, using memory optimizations that allow it to run on mobile phones to full servers.
  - branch/tag used: v0.12.0 Release Candidate tag
  - Justification: Stable and well tested
  - Source_Directories:
    - /home/ubuntu/src/mxnet
- Caffe2: Caffe2 is a cross-platform framework made with expression, speed, and modularity in mind.
  - branch/tag used: v0.8.1 tag
  - Justification: Stable and well tested
  - Note: Available for Python2.7 only
  - Source_Directories:
    - For Python2.7+ - /home/ec2-user/src/caffe2
    - For Anaconda Python2.7+ - /home/ec2-user/src/caffe2_anaconda2
- TensorFlow: TensorFlow™ is an open source software library for numerical computation using data flow graphs.
  - branch/tag used : Master tag
  - Justification : Stable and well tested
  - Source_Directories :
    - For Python2.7+ - /home/ubuntu/src/caffe
    - For Python3+ - /home/ubuntu/src/caffe3

- For Anaconda Python2.7+ - /home/ubuntu/src/caffe_anaconda2
- For Anaconda3 Python3+ - /home/ubuntu/src/caffe_anaconda3
- For CPU_ONLY : /home/ubuntu/src/caffe_cpu

Python 2.7 and Python 3.5 Support

Python 2.7 and Python 3.5 are supported in the AMI for the following Deep Learning Frameworks:

1. MXNet
2. Caffe2
3. Tensorflow

CPU Instance Type Support

The AMI supports CPU Instance Types for all frameworks. MXNet is built with support for Intel MKL2017 DNN library support.

GPU Drivers Installed

- CuDNN 7
- Nvidia 384.81
- CUDA 9.0

Launching Deep Learning Instance

Choose the flavor of the AMI from the list below in the region of your choice and follow the steps at:

EC2 Documentation to launch P2 Instance

Testing the FrameWorks

The Deep Learning frameworks have been tested with MNIST data. The AMI contains scripts to train and test with MNIST for each of the frameworks.

The scripts are available in the /home/ubuntu/src/bin directory.

The following scripts test the various frameworks:

/home/ubuntu/src/bin/testMXNet : tests MXNet

/home/ubuntu/src/bin/testTensorFlow : tests TensorFlow

/home/ubuntu/src/bin/testCaffe2 : tests Caffe2

The following tests have been run against each of the frameworks:

- MXNet: This example inside the MXNet repository. Validation accuracy threshold tested for is 97%.
- Tensorflow: This example inside the keras repository. Validation accuracy threshold tested for is 95%.
- Caffe2: Based on this example inside the Caffe2 repository. Validation accuracy threshold is 90%.

Ubuntu AMI

Ubuntu based Deep Learning AMIs are available in the following regions:

- eu-west-1(DUB)
- us-east-1(IAD)
- us-west-1(PDX)
- us-east-2(CHM)
- ap-southeast-2(SYD)
- ap-northeast-1(NRT)
- ap-northeast-2(ICN)

References

MXNet

Test Environments

- Built on p2.16xlarge.
- Also tested on p2.xlarge, c4.4xlarge.

Known Issues

- **Issue**: Tutorials provided by the framework or third parties may have Python dependencies not installed on the DLAMI.

  Workaround: You will need to install those while in the activated environment with conda or pip.

- **Issue**: Module not found error running Caffe2 examples.

  Workaround: Caffe2 optional dependencies are needed for some tutorials

- **Issue**: Caffe2 model download features result in 404. The models have changed locations since the v0.8.1 release. Update models/download.py to use the update from master.

- **Issue**: matplotlib can only render png.

  Workaround: Install Pillow then restart your kernel.

- **Issue**: Changing Caffe2 source code doesn't seem to work.

  Workaround: Change your PYTHONPATH to use the install location `/usr/local/caffe2` instead of the build folder.

- **Issue**: Caffe2 net_drawer errors.

  Workaround: Use the logger patch found in this commit.

- **Issue**: Caffe2 example shows an error regarding LMDB (can't open DB, etc.)

  Workaround: This will require a build from source after installing system LMDB, such as: `sudo apt-get install liblmdb-dev`

- **Issue**: SSH disconnects while using Jupyter server ties up your local port. When trying create a tunnel to the server you see `channel_setup_fwd_listener_tcpip: cannot listen to port: 8157`.

  Workaround: Use `lsof -ti:8057 | xargs kill -9` where 8057 is the local port you used. Then try to create the tunnel to your Jupyter server again.

Deep Learning AMI Ubuntu Version: 2.3_Sep2017

Deep Learning Amazon Machine Image

The Deep Learning AMIs are pre-built with popular Deep Learning frameworks and also contain the Anaconda Platform (Python2 and Python3).

Highlights of the Release

1. Used Ubuntu 16.04 (ami-d15a75c7) as the base AMI

2. CUDA 8 support

3. Framework upgrades for Tensorflow(v1.3.0), Caffe2(v0.8.0), Caffe(1.0), CNTK(v2.0), Theano(rel-0.9.0)

Pre-built Deep Learning Frameworks

- MXNet: MXNet is a flexible, efficient, portable and scalable open source library for deep learning. It supports declarative and imperative programming models, across a wide variety of programming languages, making it powerful yet simple to code deep learning applications. MXNet is efficient, inherently supporting automatic parallel scheduling of portions of source code that can be parallelized over a distributed environment. MXNet is also portable, using memory optimizations that allow it to run on mobile phones to full servers.

    - branch/tag used: v0.11.0 tag

    - Justification: Stable and well tested

    - Source_Directories:

        - /home/ubuntu/src/mxnet

- Caffe: Caffe is a deep learning framework made with expression, speed, and modularity in mind. It is developed by the Berkeley Vision and Learning Center (BVLC) and by community contributors.

    - branch/tag used: v1.0 tag

    - Justification: Supports cuda8.0 and cudnn 5.1

    - Source_Directories:

        - For Python2.7+ - /home/ubuntu/src/caffe

        - For Python3+ - /home/ubuntu/src/caffe3

        - For Anaconda Python2.7+ - /home/ubuntu/src/caffe_anaconda2

        - For Anaconda3 Python3+ - /home/ubuntu/src/caffe_anaconda3

        - For CPU_ONLY : /home/ubuntu/src/caffe_cpu

- Caffe2: Caffe2 is a cross-platform framework made with expression, speed, and modularity in mind.

    - branch/tag used: v0.8.0 tag

    - Justification: Stable and well tested

    - Note: This is an experimental release and there may be some issues. Available for Python2.7 only

    - Source_Directories:

        - For Python2.7+ - /home/ubuntu/src/caffe2

- For Anaconda Python2.7+ - /home/ubuntu/src/caffe2_anaconda2
- Theano: Theano is a Python library that allows you to define, optimize, and evaluate mathematical expressions involving multi-dimensional arrays efficiently.
  - branch/tag used: rel-0.9.0 tag
  - Justification: Stable and well tested
  - Source_Directories:
    - /home/ubuntu/src/Theano
- TensorFlow: TensorFlow™ is an open source software library for numerical computation using data flow graphs.
  - branch/tag used : v1.3.0 tag
  - Justification : Stable and well tested
  - Source_Directories :
    - For Python2.7+ - /home/ubuntu/src/tensorflow
    - For Python3+ - /home/ubuntu/src/tensorflow3
    - For Anaconda Python2.7+ - /home/ubuntu/src/tensorflow_anaconda
    - For Anaconda Python3+ - /home/ubuntu/src/tensorflow_anaconda3
- Torch: Torch is a scientific computing framework with wide support for machine learning algorithms that puts GPUs first. It is easy to use and efficient, thanks to an easy and fast scripting language, LuaJIT, and an underlying C/CUDA implementation.
  - branch/tag used : master branch
  - Justification : No other stable branch or tag available
  - Source_Directories :
    - /home/ubuntu/src/torch
- CNTK: CNTK - Microsoft Cognitive Toolkit - is a unified deep-learning toolkit by Microsoft Research.
  - branch/tag used : v2.0 tag
  - Justification : Stable release
  - Source_Directories :
    - /home/ubuntu/src/cntk
- Keras: Keras - Deep Learning Library for Python)
  - branch/tag used : master (with MXNet support)
  - Justification : Stable release (1.2.2)
  - Source_Directories:
    - /home/ubuntu/src/keras

Python 2.7 and Python 3.5 Support

Python 2.7 and Python 3.5 are supported in the AMI for the following Deep Learning Frameworks:

1. Caffe
2. Tensorflow

3. Theano

4. MXNet

5. CNTK

CPU Instance Type Support

The AMI supports CPU Instance Types for all frameworks. MXNet is built with support for Intel MKL2017 DNN library support. If you want to use the caffe binary for the CPU instance, then you should use the binary inside /home/ubuntu/src/caffe_cpu/

CNTK Python Support

You can run CNTK for Python inside a conda environment. To do this:

```
1  cd /home/ubuntu/src/anaconda3/bin
2          source activate cntk-py34
```

GPU Drivers Installed

- CuDNN 5.1

- NVIDIA 375.66

- CUDA 8.0

Launching Deep Learning Instance

Choose the flavor of the AMI from the list below in the region of your choice and follow the steps at:

EC2 Documentation to launch P2 Instance

Testing the Frameworks

The Deep Learning frameworks have been tested with MNIST data. The AMI contains scripts to train and test with MNIST for each of the frameworks. The test checks if the validation accuracy is above a specific threshold. The threshold is different for each of the frameworks.

The scripts are available in the /home/ubuntu/src/bin directory.

The following scripts test the various frameworks:

/home/ubuntu/src/bin/testAll : tests all frameworks

/home/ubuntu/src/bin/testMXNet : tests MXNet

/home/ubuntu/src/bin/testTheano : tests Theano

/home/ubuntu/src/bin/testTensorFlow : tests TensorFlow

/home/ubuntu/src/bin/testTorch : tests Torch

/home/ubuntu/src/bin/testCNTK : tests CNTK

/home/ubuntu/src/bin/testCaffe2 : tests Caffe2

The following tests have been run against each of the frameworks:

- MXNet: This example inside the MXNet repository. Validation accuracy threshold tested for is 97%.

- Tensorflow: This example inside the keras repository. Validation accuracy threshold tested for is 95%.

- Theano: The same example above. Validation accuracy threshold is 95%.

- Torch: This example inside the Torch tree. Validation accuracy threshold is 93%.

- Caffe: This example inside the Caffe repository. Validation accuracy threshold is 98%.

- CNTK: This example inside the CNTK repository. Validation accuracy threshold is 97%.

- Caffe2: Based on this example inside the Caffe2 repository. Validation accuracy threshold is 90%.

Ubuntu AMI

Ubuntu based Deep Learning AMIs are available in the following regions:

- eu-west-1(DUB)

- us-east-1(IAD)

- us-west-1(PDX)

- us-east-2(CHM)

- ap-southeast-2(SYD)

- ap-northeast-1(NRT)

- ap-northeast-2(ICN)

References

MXNet

Caffe

Theano

TensorFlow

Torch

CNTK

Test Environments

- Built on p2.16xlarge.

- Also tested on p2.xlarge, p2.8xlarge, p2.16xlarge, c4.4xlarge.

Known Issues

- Need to use sudo to run the testCNTK script.

  e.g. sudo ./testCNTK

Not Supported

- Functioning of multiple frameworks together in the same Python process has not been tested.

  For example, a code snippet like the following:

```
1 import mxnet as mx
2          import tensorflow as tf
```

  in the same Python process may cause an issue.

Deep Learning AMI Ubuntu Version: 2.2_August2017

Deep Learning Amazon Machine Image

The Deep Learning AMIs are pre-built with popular Deep Learning frameworks and also contain the Anaconda Platform (Python2 and Python3).

Highlights of the Release

1. Used Ubuntu 16.04 (ami-d15a75c7) as the base AMI
2. CUDA 8 support
3. Framework upgrades for Tensorflow(v1.2.0), Caffe2(v0.7.0), Caffe(1.0), CNTK(v2.0), Theano(rel-0.9.0)

Pre-built Deep Learning Frameworks

- MXNet: MXNet is a flexible, efficient, portable and scalable open source library for deep learning. It supports declarative and imperative programming models, across a wide variety of programming languages, making it powerful yet simple to code deep learning applications. MXNet is efficient, inherently supporting automatic parallel scheduling of portions of source code that can be parallelized over a distributed environment. MXNet is also portable, using memory optimizations that allow it to run on mobile phones to full servers.
    - branch/tag used: v0.10.0 tag
    - Justification: Stable and well tested
    - Source_Directories:
        - /home/ubuntu/src/mxnet
- Caffe: Caffe is a deep learning framework made with expression, speed, and modularity in mind. It is developed by the Berkeley Vision and Learning Center (BVLC) and by community contributors.
    - branch/tag used: v1.0 tag
    - Justification: Supports cuda8.0 and cudnn 5.1
    - Source_Directories:
        - For Python2.7+ - /home/ubuntu/src/caffe
        - For Python3+ - /home/ubuntu/src/caffe3
        - For Anaconda Python2.7+ - /home/ubuntu/src/caffe_anaconda2
        - For Anaconda3 Python3+ - /home/ubuntu/src/caffe_anaconda3
        - For CPU_ONLY : /home/ubuntu/src/caffe_cpu
- Caffe2: Caffe2 is a cross-platform framework made with expression, speed, and modularity in mind.
    - branch/tag used: v0.7.0 tag
    - Justification: Pre-release
    - Note: This is an experimental release and there may be some issues. Available for Python2.7 only
    - Source_Directories:
        - For Python2.7+ - /home/ubuntu/src/caffe2

- For Anaconda Python2.7+ - /home/ubuntu/src/caffe2_anaconda2

- Theano: Theano is a Python library that allows you to define, optimize, and evaluate mathematical expressions involving multi-dimensional arrays efficiently.

  - branch/tag used: rel-0.9.0 tag

  - Justification: Stable and well tested

  - Source_Directories:

    - /home/ubuntu/src/Theano

- TensorFlow: TensorFlow™ is an open source software library for numerical computation using data flow graphs.

  - branch/tag used : v1.2.0 tag

  - Justification : Stable and well tested

  - Source_Directories :

    - For Python2.7+ - /home/ubuntu/src/tensorflow

    - For Python3+ - /home/ubuntu/src/tensorflow3

    - For Anaconda Python2.7+ - /home/ubuntu/src/tensorflow_anaconda

    - For Anaconda Python3+ - /home/ubuntu/src/tensorflow_anaconda3

- Torch: Torch is a scientific computing framework with wide support for machine learning algorithms that puts GPUs first. It is easy to use and efficient, thanks to an easy and fast scripting language, LuaJIT, and an underlying C/CUDA implementation.

  - branch/tag used : master branch

  - Justification : No other stable branch or tag available

  - Source_Directories :

    - /home/ubuntu/src/torch

- CNTK: CNTK - Microsoft Cognitive Toolkit - is a unified deep-learning toolkit by Microsoft Research.

  - branch/tag used : v2.0 tag

  - Justification : Latest release

  - Source_Directories :

    - /home/ubuntu/src/cntk

- Keras: Keras - Deep Learning Library for Python)

  - branch/tag used : 1.2.2 tag

  - Justification : Stable release

  - Source_Directories:

    - /home/ubuntu/src/keras

Python 2.7 and Python 3.5 Support

Python 2.7 and Python 3.5 are supported in the AMI for the following Deep Learning Frameworks:

1. Caffe

2. Tensorflow

139

3. Theano

4. MXNet

5. CNTK

CPU Instance Type Support

The AMI supports CPU Instance Types for all frameworks. MXNet is built with support for Intel MKL2017 DNN library support. If you want to use the caffe binary for the CPU instance, then you should use the binary inside /home/ubuntu/src/caffe_cpu/

CNTK Python Support

You can run CNTK for Python inside a conda environment. To do this:

```
1 cd /home/ubuntu/src/anaconda3/bin
2         source activate cntk-py34
```

GPU Drivers Installed

- CuDNN 5.1

- NVIDIA 375.66

- CUDA 8.0

Launching Deep Learning Instance

Choose the flavor of the AMI from the list below in the region of your choice and follow the steps at:

EC2 Documentation to launch G2 Instance

Testing the Frameworks

The Deep Learning frameworks have been tested with MNIST data. The AMI contains scripts to train and test with MNIST for each of the frameworks. The test checks if the validation accuracy is above a specific threshold. The threshold is different for each of the frameworks.

The scripts are available in the /home/ec2-user/src/bin directory.

The following scripts test the various frameworks:

/home/ubuntu/src/bin/testAll : tests all frameworks

/home/ubuntu/src/bin/testMXNet : tests MXNet

/home/ubuntu/src/bin/testTheano : tests Theano

/home/ubuntu/src/bin/testTensorFlow : tests TensorFlow

/home/ubuntu/src/bin/testTorch : tests Torch

/home/ubuntu/src/bin/testCNTK : tests CNTK

/home/ubuntu/src/bin/testCaffe2 : tests Caffe2

The following tests have been run against each of the frameworks:

- MXNet: This example inside the MXNet repository. Validation accuracy threshold tested for is 97%.

- Tensorflow: This example inside the keras repository. Validation accuracy threshold tested for is 95%.

- Theano: The same example above. Validation accuracy threshold is 95%.

- Torch: This example inside the Torch tree. Validation accuracy threshold is 93%.

- Caffe: This example inside the Caffe repository. Validation accuracy threshold is 98%.

- CNTK: This example inside the CNTK repository. Validation accuracy threshold is 97%.

- Caffe2: Based on this example inside the Caffe2 repository. Validation accuracy threshold is 90%.

Ubuntu AMI

Ubuntu based Deep Learning AMIs are available in the following regions:

- eu-west-1(DUB)

- us-east-1(IAD)

- us-west-1(PDX)

- us-east-2(CHM)

- ap-southeast-2(SYD)

- ap-northeast-1(NRT)

- ap-northeast-2(ICN)

References

MXNet

Caffe

Theano

TensorFlow

Torch

CNTK

Test Environments

- Built on p2.16xlarge.

- Also tested on g2.2xlarge, g2.8xlarge, p2.xlarge, p2.8xlarge, p2.16xlarge, c4.4xlarge.

Known Issues

- Need to use sudo to run the testCNTK script.

  e.g. sudo ./testCNTK

Not Supported

- Functioning of multiple frameworks together in the same Python process has not been tested.
  For example, a code snippet like the following:

```python
import mxnet as mx
        import tensorflow as tf
```

in the same Python process may cause an issue.

Deep Learning AMI Ubuntu Version: 1.5_June2017

Deep Learning Amazon Machine Image

The Deep Learning AMIs are pre-built with popular Deep Learning frameworks and also contain the Anaconda Platform (Python2 and Python3).

Highlights of the Release

1. MXNet compiled with S3 Support(USE_S3=1).
2. Used the latest base AMI for Ubuntu 14.04 (ami-b1143ba7).

Pre-built Deep Learning Frameworks

- MXNet: MXNet is a flexible, efficient, portable and scalable open source library for deep learning. It supports declarative and imperative programming models, across a wide variety of programming languages, making it powerful yet simple to code deep learning applications. MXNet is efficient, inherently supporting automatic parallel scheduling of portions of source code that can be parallelized over a distributed environment. MXNet is also portable, using memory optimizations that allow it to run on mobile phones to full servers.
  - branch/tag used: v0.10.0 tag
  - Justification: Stable and well tested
  - Source_Directories:
    - /home/ubuntu/src/mxnet
- Caffe: Caffe is a deep learning framework made with expression, speed, and modularity in mind. It is developed by the Berkeley Vision and Learning Center (BVLC) and by community contributors.
  - branch/tag used: rc5 tag
  - Justification: Supports cuda7.5 and cudnn 5.1
  - Source_Directories:
    - For Python2.7+ - /home/ubuntu/src/caffe
    - For Python3+ - /home/ubuntu/src/caffe3
    - For Anaconda Python2.7+ - /home/ubuntu/src/caffe_anaconda2
    - For Anaconda3 Python3+ - /home/ubuntu/src/caffe_anaconda3
    - For CPU_ONLY : /home/ubuntu/src/caffe_cpu
- Caffe2: Caffe2 is a cross-platform framework made with expression, speed, and modularity in mind.
  - branch/tag used: v0.7.0 tag
  - Justification: Pre-release
  - Note: This is an experimental release and there may be some issues. Available for Python2.7 only
  - Source_Directories:
    - For Python2.7+ - /home/ubuntu/src/caffe2
    - For Anaconda Python2.7+ - /home/ubuntu/src/caffe2_anaconda2

- Theano: Theano is a Python library that allows you to define, optimize, and evaluate mathematical expressions involving multi-dimensional arrays efficiently.
  - branch/tag used: rel-0.9.0 tag
  - Justification: Stable and well tested
  - Source_Directories:
    - /home/ubuntu/src/Theano
- TensorFlow: TensorFlow™ is an open source software library for numerical computation using data flow graphs.
  - branch/tag used : v1.1.0 tag
  - Justification : Stable and well tested
  - Source_Directories :
    - For Python2.7+ - /home/ubuntu/src/tensorflow
    - For Python3+ - /home/ubuntu/src/tensorflow3
    - For Anaconda Python2.7+ - /home/ubuntu/src/tensorflow_anaconda
    - For Anaconda Python3+ - /home/ubuntu/src/tensorflow_anaconda3
- Torch: Torch is a scientific computing framework with wide support for machine learning algorithms that puts GPUs first. It is easy to use and efficient, thanks to an easy and fast scripting language, LuaJIT, and an underlying C/CUDA implementation.
  - branch/tag used : master branch
  - Justification : No other stable branch or tag available
  - Source_Directories :
    - /home/ubuntu/src/torch
- CNTK: CNTK - Microsoft Cognitive Toolkit - is a unified deep-learning toolkit by Microsoft Research.
  - branch/tag used : v2.0.rc1 tag
  - Justification : Latest release
  - Source_Directories :
    - /home/ubuntu/src/cntk
- Keras: Keras - Deep Learning Library for Python)
  - branch/tag used : 1.2.2 tag
  - Justification : Stable release
  - Source_Directories:
    - /home/ubuntu/src/keras

Python 2.7 and Python 3.5 Support

Python 2.7 and Python 3.5 are supported in the AMI for the following Deep Learning Frameworks:

1. Caffe
2. Tensorflow
3. Theano

4. MXNet

5. CNTK

CPU Instance Type Support

The AMI supports CPU Instance Types for all frameworks. MXNet is built with support for Intel MKL2017 DNN library support. If you want to use the caffe binary for the CPU instance, then you should use the binary inside /home/ubuntu/src/caffe_cpu/

CNTK Python Support

You can run CNTK for Python inside a conda environment. To do this:

```
1  cd /home/ubuntu/src/anaconda3/bin
2        source activate cntk-py34
```

GPU Drivers Installed

- CuDNN 5.1
- NVIDIA 367.57
- CUDA 7.5

Launching Deep Learning Instance

Choose the flavor of the AMI from the list below in the region of your choice and follow the steps at:

EC2 Documentation to launch G2 Instance

Testing the Frameworks

The Deep Learning frameworks have been tested with MNIST data. The AMI contains scripts to train and test with MNIST for each of the frameworks. The test checks if the validation accuracy is above a specific threshold. The threshold is different for each of the frameworks.

The scripts are available in the /home/ec2-user/src/bin directory.

The following scripts test the various frameworks:

/home/ubuntu/src/bin/testAll : tests all frameworks

/home/ubuntu/src/bin/testMXNet : tests MXNet

/home/ubuntu/src/bin/testTheano : tests Theano

/home/ubuntu/src/bin/testTensorFlow : tests TensorFlow

/home/ubuntu/src/bin/testTorch : tests Torch

/home/ubuntu/src/bin/testCNTK : tests CNTK

/home/ubuntu/src/bin/testCaffe2 : tests Caffe2

The following tests have been run against each of the frameworks:

- MXNet: This example inside the MXNet repository. Validation accuracy threshold tested for is 97%.

- Tensorflow: This example inside the keras repository. Validation accuracy threshold tested for is 95%.

- Theano: The same example above. Validation accuracy threshold is 95%.

- Torch: This example inside the Torch tree. Validation accuracy threshold is 93%.

- Caffe: This example inside the Caffe repository. Validation accuracy threshold is 98%.

- CNTK: This example inside the CNTK repository. Validation accuracy threshold is 97%.

- Caffe2: Based on this example inside the Caffe2 repository. Validation accuracy threshold is 90%.

Ubuntu AMI

Ubuntu based Deep Learning AMIs are available in the following regions:

- eu-west-1(DUB)

- us-east-1(IAD)

- us-west-1(PDX)

- us-east-2(CHM)

- ap-southeast-2(SYD)

- ap-northeast-1(NRT)

- ap-northeast-2(ICN)

References

MXNet

Caffe

Theano

TensorFlow

Torch

CNTK

Test Environments

- Built on p2.16xlarge.

- Also tested on g2.2xlarge, g2.8xlarge, p2.xlarge, p2.8xlarge, p2.16xlarge, c4.4xlarge.

Known Issues

- Need to use sudo to run the testCNTK script.

  e.g. sudo ./testCNTK

- There is a known issue with the Dropout operator when running on GPU instance types. Please see the Github Issue for details and workaround.

Not Supported

- Functioning of multiple frameworks together in the same Python process has not been tested. For example, a code snippet like the following:

```
1 import mxnet as mx
2         import tensorflow as tf
```

in the same Python process may cause an issue.

Deep Learning AMI Ubuntu Version: 1.4_June2017

Deep Learning Amazon Machine Image

The Deep Learning AMIs are pre-built with popular Deep Learning frameworks and also contain the Anaconda Platform (Python2 and Python3).

Pre-built Deep Learning Frameworks

- MXNet: MXNet is a flexible, efficient, portable and scalable open source library for deep learning. It supports declarative and imperative programming models, across a wide variety of programming languages, making it powerful yet simple to code deep learning applications. MXNet is efficient, inherently supporting automatic parallel scheduling of portions of source code that can be parallelized over a distributed environment. MXNet is also portable, using memory optimizations that allow it to run on mobile phones to full servers.

  - branch/tag used: v0.10.0 tag
  - Justification: Stable and well tested
  - Source_Directories:
    - /home/ubuntu/src/mxnet

- Caffe: Caffe is a deep learning framework made with expression, speed, and modularity in mind. It is developed by the Berkeley Vision and Learning Center (BVLC) and by community contributors.

  - branch/tag used: rc5 tag
  - Justification: Supports cuda7.5 and cudnn 5.1
  - Source_Directories:
    - For Python2.7+ - /home/ubuntu/src/caffe
    - For Python3+ - /home/ubuntu/src/caffe3
    - For Anaconda Python2.7+ - /home/ubuntu/src/caffe_anaconda2
    - For Anaconda3 Python3+ - /home/ubuntu/src/caffe_anaconda3
    - For CPU_ONLY : /home/ubuntu/src/caffe_cpu

- Caffe2: Caffe2 is a cross-platform framework made with expression, speed, and modularity in mind.

  - branch/tag used: v0.7.0 tag
  - Justification: Pre-release
  - Note: This is an experimental release and there may be some issues. Available for Python2.7 only
  - Source_Directories:
    - For Python2.7+ - /home/ubuntu/src/caffe2
    - For Anaconda Python2.7+ - /home/ubuntu/src/caffe2_anaconda2

- Theano: Theano is a Python library that allows you to define, optimize, and evaluate mathematical expressions involving multi-dimensional arrays efficiently.

  - branch/tag used: rel-0.9.0 tag
  - Justification: Stable and well tested
  - Source_Directories:

- /home/ubuntu/src/Theano
- TensorFlow: TensorFlow™ is an open source software library for numerical computation using data flow graphs.
  - branch/tag used : v1.1.0 tag
  - Justification : Stable and well tested
  - Source_Directories :
    - For Python2.7+ - /home/ubuntu/src/tensorflow
    - For Python3+ - /home/ubuntu/src/tensorflow3
    - For Anaconda Python2.7+ - /home/ubuntu/src/tensorflow_anaconda
    - For Anaconda Python3+ - /home/ubuntu/src/tensorflow_anaconda3
- Torch: Torch is a scientific computing framework with wide support for machine learning algorithms that puts GPUs first. It is easy to use and efficient, thanks to an easy and fast scripting language, LuaJIT, and an underlying C/CUDA implementation.
  - branch/tag used : master branch
  - Justification : No other stable branch or tag available
  - Source_Directories :
    - /home/ubuntu/src/torch
- CNTK: CNTK - Microsoft Cognitive Toolkit - is a unified deep-learning toolkit by Microsoft Research.
  - branch/tag used : v2.0.rc1 tag
  - Justification : Latest release
  - Source_Directories :
    - /home/ubuntu/src/cntk
- Keras: Keras - Deep Learning Library for Python)
  - branch/tag used : 1.2.2 tag
  - Justification : Stable release
  - Source_Directories:
    - /home/ubuntu/src/keras

Python 2.7 and Python 3.5 Support

Python 2.7 and Python 3.5 are supported in the AMI for the following Deep Learning Frameworks:

1. Caffe
2. Tensorflow
3. Theano
4. MXNet
5. CNTK

CPU Instance Type Support

The AMI supports CPU Instance Types for all frameworks. MXNet is built with support for Intel MKL2017 DNN library support. If you want to use the caffe binary for the CPU instance, then you should use the binary inside /home/ubuntu/src/caffe_cpu/

CNTK Python Support

You can run CNTK for Python inside a conda environment. To do this:

```
1 cd /home/ubuntu/src/anaconda3/bin
2         source activate cntk-py34
```

GPU Drivers Installed

- CuDNN 5.1
- NVIDIA 367.57
- CUDA 7.5

Launching Deep Learning Instance

Choose the flavor of the AMI from the list below in the region of your choice and follow the steps at:

EC2 Documentation to launch G2 Instance

Testing the Frameworks

The Deep Learning frameworks have been tested with MNIST data. The AMI contains scripts to train and test with MNIST for each of the frameworks. The test checks if the validation accuracy is above a specific threshold. The threshold is different for each of the frameworks.

The scripts are available in the /home/ec2-user/src/bin directory.

The following scripts test the various frameworks:

/home/ubuntu/src/bin/testAll : tests all frameworks

/home/ubuntu/src/bin/testMXNet : tests MXNet

/home/ubuntu/src/bin/testTheano : tests Theano

/home/ubuntu/src/bin/testTensorFlow : tests TensorFlow

/home/ubuntu/src/bin/testTorch : tests Torch

/home/ubuntu/src/bin/testCNTK : tests CNTK

/home/ubuntu/src/bin/testCaffe2 : tests Caffe2

The following tests have been run against each of the frameworks:

- MXNet: This example inside the MXNet repository. Validation accuracy threshold tested for is 97%.
- Tensorflow: This example inside the keras repository. Validation accuracy threshold tested for is 95%.
- Theano: The same example above. Validation accuracy threshold is 95%.
- Torch: This example inside the Torch tree. Validation accuracy threshold is 93%.

- Caffe: This example inside the Caffe repository. Validation accuracy threshold is 98%.

- CNTK: This example inside the CNTK repository. Validation accuracy threshold is 97%.

- Caffe2: Based on this example inside the Caffe2 repository. Validation accuracy threshold is 90%.

Ubuntu AMI

Ubuntu based Deep Learning AMIs are available in the following regions:

- eu-west-1(DUB)

- us-east-1(IAD)

- us-west-1(PDX)

- us-east-2(CHM)

- ap-southeast-2(SYD)

- ap-northeast-1(NRT)

- ap-northeast-2(ICN)

References

MXNet

Caffe

Theano

TensorFlow

Torch

CNTK

Test Environments

- Built on p2.16xlarge.

- Also tested on g2.2xlarge, g2.8xlarge, p2.xlarge, p2.8xlarge, p2.16xlarge, c4.4xlarge.

Known Issues

- Need to use sudo to run the testCNTK script.

  e.g. sudo ./testCNTK

- There is a known issue with the Dropout operator when running on GPU instance types. Please see the Github Issue for details and workaround.

Not Supported

- Functioning of multiple frameworks together in the same Python process has not been tested. For example, a code snippet like the following:

```
1 import mxnet as mx
2          import tensorflow as tf
```

in the same Python process may cause an issue.

Deep Learning AMI Ubuntu Version: 1.3_Apr2017

Deep Learning Amazon Machine Image

The Deep Learning AMIs are pre-built with popular Deep Learning frameworks and also contain the Anaconda Platform (Python2 and Python3).

Pre-built Deep Learning Frameworks

- MXNet: MXNet is a flexible, efficient, portable and scalable open source library for deep learning. It supports declarative and imperative programming models, across a wide variety of programming languages, making it powerful yet simple to code deep learning applications. MXNet is efficient, inherently supporting automatic parallel scheduling of portions of source code that can be parallelized over a distributed environment. MXNet is also portable, using memory optimizations that allow it to run on mobile phones to full servers.

  - branch/tag used: v0.9.3 tag

  - Justification: Stable and well tested

  - Source_Directories:

    - /home/ubuntu/src/mxnet

- Caffe: Caffe is a deep learning framework made with expression, speed, and modularity in mind. It is developed by the Berkeley Vision and Learning Center (BVLC) and by community contributors.

  - branch/tag used: rc5 tag

  - Justification: Supports cuda7.5 and cudnn 5.1

  - Source_Directories:

    - For Python2.7+ - /home/ubuntu/src/caffe

    - For Python3+ - /home/ubuntu/src/caffe3

    - For Anaconda Python2.7+ - /home/ubuntu/src/caffe_anaconda2

    - For Anaconda3 Python3+ - /home/ubuntu/src/caffe_anaconda3

    - For CPU_ONLY : /home/ubuntu/src/caffe_cpu

- Caffe2: Caffe2 is a cross-platform framework made with expression, speed, and modularity in mind.

  - branch/tag used: v0.6.0 tag

  - Justification: Pre-release

  - Note: This is an experimental release and there may be some issues. Available for Python2.7 only

  - Source_Directories:

    - For Python2.7+ - /home/ubuntu/src/caffe2

    - For Anaconda Python2.7+ - /home/ubuntu/src/caffe2_anaconda2

- Theano: Theano is a Python library that allows you to define, optimize, and evaluate mathematical expressions involving multi-dimensional arrays efficiently.

  - branch/tag used: rel-0.8.2 tag

  - Justification: Stable and well tested

  - Source_Directories:

- /home/ubuntu/src/Theano

- TensorFlow: TensorFlow™ is an open source software library for numerical computation using data flow graphs.

  - branch/tag used : v1.0.1 tag

  - Justification : Stable and well tested

  - Source_Directories :

    - For Python2.7+ - /home/ubuntu/src/tensorflow

    - For Python3+ - /home/ubuntu/src/tensorflow3

    - For Anaconda Python2.7+ - /home/ubuntu/src/tensorflow_anaconda

    - For Anaconda Python3+ - /home/ubuntu/src/tensorflow_anaconda3

- Torch: Torch is a scientific computing framework with wide support for machine learning algorithms that puts GPUs first. It is easy to use and efficient, thanks to an easy and fast scripting language, LuaJIT, and an underlying C/CUDA implementation.

  - branch/tag used : master branch

  - Justification : No other stable branch or tag available

  - Source_Directories :

    - /home/ubuntu/src/torch

- CNTK: CNTK - Microsoft Cognitive Toolkit - is a unified deep-learning toolkit by Microsoft Research.

  - branch/tag used : v2.0.rc1 tag

  - Justification : Latest release

  - Source_Directories :

    - /home/ubuntu/src/cntk

- Keras: Keras - Deep Learning Library for Python)

  - branch/tag used : 1.2.2 tag

  - Justification : Stable release

  - Source_Directories:

    - /home/ubuntu/src/keras

Python 2.7 and Python 3.5 Support

Python 2.7 and Python 3.5 are supported in the AMI for the following Deep Learning Frameworks:

1. Caffe

2. Tensorflow

3. Theano

4. MXNet

5. CNTK

CPU Instance Type Support

The AMI supports CPU Instance Types for all frameworks. MXNet is built with support for Intel MKL2017 DNN library support. If you want to use the caffe binary for the CPU instance, then you should use the binary inside /home/ubuntu/src/caffe_cpu/

CNTK Python Support

You can run CNTK for Python inside a conda environment. To do this:

```
1 cd /home/ubuntu/src/anaconda3/bin
2       source activate cntk-py34
```

GPU Drivers Installed

- CuDNN 5.1
- NVIDIA 367.57
- CUDA 7.5

Launching Deep Learning Instance

Choose the flavor of the AMI from the list below in the region of your choice and follow the steps at:

EC2 Documentation to launch G2 Instance

Testing the Frameworks

The Deep Learning frameworks have been tested with MNIST data. The AMI contains scripts to train and test with MNIST for each of the frameworks. The test checks if the validation accuracy is above a specific threshold. The threshold is different for each of the frameworks.

The scripts are available in the /home/ec2-user/src/bin directory.

The following scripts test the various frameworks:

/home/ubuntu/src/bin/testAll : tests all frameworks

/home/ubuntu/src/bin/testMXNet : tests MXNet

/home/ubuntu/src/bin/testTheano : tests Theano

/home/ubuntu/src/bin/testTensorFlow : tests TensorFlow

/home/ubuntu/src/bin/testTorch : tests Torch

/home/ubuntu/src/bin/testCNTK : tests CNTK

/home/ubuntu/src/bin/testCaffe2 : tests Caffe2

The following tests have been run against each of the frameworks:

- MXNet: This example inside the MXNet repository. Validation accuracy threshold tested for is 97%.
- Tensorflow: This example inside the keras repository. Validation accuracy threshold tested for is 95%.
- Theano: The same example above. Validation accuracy threshold is 95%.
- Torch: This example inside the Torch tree. Validation accuracy threshold is 93%.

- Caffe: This example inside the Caffe repository. Validation accuracy threshold is 98%.
- CNTK: This example inside the CNTK repository. Validation accuracy threshold is 97%.
- Caffe2: Based on this example inside the Caffe2 repository. Validation accuracy threshold is 90%.

Ubuntu AMI

Ubuntu based Deep Learning AMIs are available in the following regions:
- eu-west-1(DUB)
- us-east-1(IAD)
- us-west-1(PDX)

References

MXNet

Caffe

Theano

TensorFlow

Torch

CNTK

Test Environments

- Built and Tested on g2.2xlarge.
- Also tested on g2.8xlarge, p2.16xlarge, c4.4xlarge.

Known Issues

- Need to use sudo to run the testCNTK script.

  e.g. sudo ./testCNTK
- There is a known issue with the Dropout operator when running on GPU instance types. Please see the Github Issue for details and workaround.

Not Supported

- Functioning of multiple frameworks together in the same Python process has not been tested.

  For example, a code snippet like the following:

```
1 import mxnet as mx
2         import tensorflow as tf
```

  in the same Python process may cause an issue.

Deep Learning AMI Ubuntu Version: 1.2

Deep Learning Amazon Machine Image

The Deep Learning AMIs are pre-built with popular Deep Learning frameworks and also contain the Anaconda Platform (Python2 and Python3).

Pre-built Deep Learning Frameworks

- MXNet: MXNet is a flexible, efficient, portable and scalable open source library for deep learning. It supports declarative and imperative programming models, across a wide variety of programming languages, making it powerful yet simple to code deep learning applications. MXNet is efficient, inherently supporting automatic parallel scheduling of portions of source code that can be parallelized over a distributed environment. MXNet is also portable, using memory optimizations that allow it to run on mobile phones to full servers.
  - branch/tag used: v0.9.3 tag
  - Justification: Stable and well tested
  - Source_Directories:
    - /home/ubuntu/src/mxnet
- Caffe: Caffe is a deep learning framework made with expression, speed, and modularity in mind. It is developed by the Berkeley Vision and Learning Center (BVLC) and by community contributors.
  - branch/tag used: rc5 tag
  - Justification: Supports cuda7.5 and cudnn 5.1
  - Source_Directories:
    - For Python2.7+ - /home/ubuntu/src/caffe
    - For Python3+ - /home/ubuntu/src/caffe3
    - For Anaconda Python2.7+ - /home/ubuntu/src/caffe_anaconda2
    - For Anaconda3 Python3+ - /home/ubuntu/src/caffe_anaconda3
    - For CPU_ONLY : /home/ubuntu/src/caffe_cpu
- Theano: Theano is a Python library that allows you to define, optimize, and evaluate mathematical expressions involving multi-dimensional arrays efficiently.
  - branch/tag used: rel-0.8.2 tag
  - Justification: Stable and well tested
  - Source_Directories:
    - /home/ubuntu/src/Theano
- TensorFlow: TensorFlow™ is an open source software library for numerical computation using data flow graphs.
  - branch/tag used : v1.0.0 tag
  - Justification : Stable and well tested
  - Source_Directories :
    - For Python2.7+ - /home/ubuntu/src/tensorflow

- For Python3+ - /home/ubuntu/src/tensorflow3

- For Anaconda Python2.7+ - /home/ubuntu/src/tensorflow_anaconda

- For Anaconda Python3+ - /home/ubuntu/src/tensorflow_anaconda3

- Torch: Torch is a scientific computing framework with wide support for machine learning algorithms that puts GPUs first. It is easy to use and efficient, thanks to an easy and fast scripting language, LuaJIT, and an underlying C/CUDA implementation.

  - branch/tag used : master branch

  - Justification : No other stable branch or tag available

  - Source_Directories :

    - /home/ubuntu/src/torch

- CNTK: CNTK - Microsoft Cognitive Toolkit - is a unified deep-learning toolkit by Microsoft Research.

  - branch/tag used : v2.0beta12.0 tag

  - Justification : Latest release

  - Source_Directories :

    - /home/ubuntu/src/cntk

- Keras: Keras - Deep Learning Library for Python)

  - branch/tag used : 1.2.2 tag

  - Justification : Stable release

  - Source_Directories:

    - /home/ubuntu/src/keras

Python 2.7 and Python 3.5 Support

Python 2.7 and Python 3.5 are supported in the AMI for the following Deep Learning Frameworks:

1. Caffe

2. Tensorflow

3. Theano

4. MXNet

5. CNTK

CPU Instance Type Support

The AMI supports CPU Instance Types for all frameworks. MXNet is built with support for Intel MKL2017 DNN library support. If you want to use the caffe binary for the CPU instance, then you should use the binary inside /home/ubuntu/src/caffe_cpu/

CNTK Python Support

You can run CNTK for Python inside a conda environment. To do this:

```
1  cd /home/ubuntu/src/anaconda3/bin
2          source activate cntk-py34
```

GPU Drivers Installed

- CuDNN 5.1
- NVIDIA 367.57
- CUDA 7.5

Launching Deep Learning Instance

Choose the flavor of the AMI from the list below in the region of your choice and follow the steps at:

EC2 Documentation to launch G2 Instance

Testing the Frameworks

The Deep Learning frameworks have been tested with MNIST data. The AMI contains scripts to train and test with MNIST for each of the frameworks. The test checks if the validation accuracy is above a specific threshold. The threshold is different for each of the frameworks.

The scripts are available in the /home/ec2-user/src/bin directory.

The following scripts test the various frameworks:

/home/ubuntu/src/bin/testAll : tests all frameworks

/home/ubuntu/src/bin/testMXNet : tests MXNet

/home/ubuntu/src/bin/testTheano : tests Theano

/home/ubuntu/src/bin/testTensorFlow : tests TensorFlow

/home/ubuntu/src/bin/testTorch : tests Torch

/home/ubuntu/src/bin/testCNTK : tests CNTK

The following tests have been run against each of the frameworks:

- MXNet: This example inside the MXNet repository. Validation accuracy threshold tested for is 97%.
- Tensorflow: This example inside the keras repository. Validation accuracy threshold tested for is 95%.
- Theano: The same example above. Validation accuracy threshold is 95%.
- Torch: This example inside the Torch tree. Validation accuracy threshold is 93%.
- Caffe: This example inside the Caffe repository. Validation accuracy threshold is 98%.
- CNTK: This example inside the CNTK repository. Validation accuracy threshold is 97%.

Ubuntu AMI

Ubuntu based Deep Learning AMIs are available in the following regions:

- eu-west-1(DUB)
- us-east-1(IAD)
- us-west-1(PDX)

References

MXNet

Caffe

Theano

TensorFlow

Torch

CNTK

Test Environments

- Built and Tested on g2.2xlarge.

- Also tested on g2.8xlarge, p2.16xlarge, c4.4xlarge.

Known Issues

- Need to use sudo to run the testCNTK script.

  e.g. sudo ./testCNTK

- There is a known issue with the Dropout operator when running on GPU instance types. Please see the Github Issue for details and workaround.

Not Supported

- Functioning of multiple frameworks together in the same Python process has not been tested.

  For example, a code snippet like the following:

```
1 import mxnet as mx
2         import tensorflow as tf
```

  in the same Python process may cause an issue.

Deep Learning AMI Ubuntu Version: 1.1

Deep Learning Amazon Machine Image

The Deep Learning AMIs are pre-built with popular Deep Learning frameworks and also contain the Anaconda Platform (Python2 and Python3).

Pre-built Deep Learning Frameworks

- MXNet: MXNet is a flexible, efficient, portable and scalable open source library for deep learning. It supports declarative and imperative programming models, across a wide variety of programming languages, making it powerful yet simple to code deep learning applications. MXNet is efficient, inherently supporting automatic parallel scheduling of portions of source code that can be parallelized over a distributed environment. MXNet is also portable, using memory optimizations that allow it to run on mobile phones to full servers.

  - branch/tag used: v0.9.3 tag
  - Justification: Stable and well tested
  - Source_Directories:
    - /home/ubuntu/src/mxnet

- Caffe: Caffe is a deep learning framework made with expression, speed, and modularity in mind. It is developed by the Berkeley Vision and Learning Center (BVLC) and by community contributors.

  - branch/tag used: rc4 tag
  - Justification: Supports cuda7.5 and cudnn 5.1
  - Source_Directories:
    - For Python2.7+ - /home/ubuntu/src/caffe
    - For Python3+ - /home/ubuntu/src/caffe3
    - For Anaconda Python2.7+ - /home/ubuntu/src/caffe_anaconda2
    - For Anaconda3 Python3+ - /home/ubuntu/src/caffe_anaconda3
    - For CPU_ONLY : /home/ubuntu/src/caffe_cpu

- Theano: Theano is a Python library that allows you to define, optimize, and evaluate mathematical expressions involving multi-dimensional arrays efficiently.

  - branch/tag used: rel-0.8.2 tag
  - Justification: Stable and well tested
  - Source_Directories:
    - /home/ubuntu/src/theano

- TensorFlow: TensorFlow™ is an open source software library for numerical computation using data flow graphs.

  - branch/tag used : v0.12.1 tag
  - Justification : Stable and well tested
  - Source_Directories :
    - For Python2.7+ - /home/ubuntu/src/tensorflow

- For Python3+ - /home/ubuntu/src/tensorflow3

- For Anaconda Python2.7+ - /home/ubuntu/src/tensorflow_anaconda

- For Anaconda Python3+ - /home/ubuntu/src/tensorflow_anaconda3

- Torch: Torch is a scientific computing framework with wide support for machine learning algorithms that puts GPUs first. It is easy to use and efficient, thanks to an easy and fast scripting language, LuaJIT, and an underlying C/CUDA implementation.

  - branch/tag used : master branch

  - Justification : No other stable branch or tag available

  - Source_Directories :

    - /home/ubuntu/src/torch

- CNTK: CNTK - Microsoft Cognitive Toolkit - is a unified deep-learning toolkit by Microsoft Research.

  - branch/tag used : v2.0beta7.0 tag

  - Justification : Latest release

  - Source_Directories :

    - /home/ubuntu/src/cntk

- Keras: Keras - Deep Learning Library for Python)

  - branch/tag used : 1.2.1 tag

  - Justification : Stable release

  - Source_Directories:

    - /home/ubuntu/src/keras

Python 2.7 and Python 3.5 Support

Python 2.7 and Python 3.5 are supported in the AMI for the following Deep Learning Frameworks:

1. Caffe

2. Tensorflow

3. Theano

4. MXNet

5. CNTK

CPU Instance Type Support

The AMI supports CPU Instance Types for all frameworks. MXNet is built with support for Intel MKL2017 DNN library support. If you want to use the caffe binary for the CPU instance, then you should use the binary inside /home/ubuntu/src/caffe_cpu/

CNTK Python Support

You can run CNTK for Python inside a conda environment. To do this:

```
1 cd /home/ubuntu/src/anaconda3/bin
2         source activate cntk-py34
```

GPU Drivers Installed

- CuDNN 5.1
- NVIDIA 352.99
- CUDA 7.5

Launching Deep Learning Instance

Choose the flavor of the AMI from the list below in the region of your choice and follow the steps at:

EC2 Documentation to launch G2 Instance

Testing the Frameworks

The Deep Learning frameworks have been tested with MNIST data. The AMI contains scripts to train and test with MNIST for each of the frameworks. The test checks if the validation accuracy is above a specific threshold. The threshold is different for each of the frameworks.

The scripts are available in the /home/ec2-user/src/bin directory.

The following scripts test the various frameworks:

/home/ubuntu/src/bin/testAll : tests all frameworks

/home/ubuntu/src/bin/testMXNet : tests MXNet

/home/ubuntu/src/bin/testTheano : tests Theano

/home/ubuntu/src/bin/testTensorFlow : tests TensorFlow

/home/ubuntu/src/bin/testTorch : tests Torch

/home/ubuntu/src/bin/testCNTK : tests CNTK

The following tests have been run against each of the frameworks:

- MXNet: This example inside the MXNet repository. Validation accuracy threshold tested for is 97%.
- Tensorflow: This example inside the keras repository. Validation accuracy threshold tested for is 95%.
- Theano: The same example above. Validation accuracy threshold is 95%.
- Torch: This example inside the Torch tree. Validation accuracy threshold is 93%.
- Caffe: This example inside the Caffe repository. Validation accuracy threshold is 98%.
- CNTK: This example inside the CNTK repository. Validation accuracy threshold is 97%.

Ubuntu AMI

Ubuntu based Deep Learning AMIs are available in the following regions:

- eu-west-1(DUB)
- us-east-1(IAD)
- us-west-1(PDX)

References

MXNet

Caffe

Theano

TensorFlow

Torch

CNTK

Test Environments

- Built and Tested on g2.2xlarge.
- Also tested on g2.8xlarge, p2.16xlarge, c4.4xlarge.

Deep Learning AMI Ubuntu Version: 1.0

Deep Learning Amazon Machine Image

The Deep Learning AMIs are pre-built with popular Deep Learning frameworks and also contain the Anaconda Platform (Python2 and Python3).

Pre-built Deep Learning Frameworks

- MXNet: MXNet is a flexible, efficient, portable and scalable open source library for deep learning. It supports declarative and imperative programming models, across a wide variety of programming languages, making it powerful yet simple to code deep learning applications. MXNet is efficient, inherently supporting automatic parallel scheduling of portions of source code that can be parallelized over a distributed environment. MXNet is also portable, using memory optimizations that allow it to run on mobile phones to full servers.

    - branch/tag used: v0.9.3 tag
    - Justification: Stable and well tested
    - Source_Directories:
        - /home/ubuntu/src/mxnet

- Caffe: Caffe is a deep learning framework made with expression, speed, and modularity in mind. It is developed by the Berkeley Vision and Learning Center (BVLC) and by community contributors.

    - branch/tag used: master branch
    - Justification: Supports cuda7.5 and cudnn 5.1
    - Source_Directories:
        - For Python2.7+ - /home/ubuntu/src/caffe
        - For Python3+ - /home/ubuntu/src/caffe3
        - For Anaconda Python2.7+ - /home/ubuntu/src/caffe_anaconda2
        - For Anaconda3 Python3+ - /home/ubuntu/src/caffe_anaconda3
        - For CPU_ONLY : /home/ubuntu/src/caffe_cpu

- Theano: Theano is a Python library that allows you to define, optimize, and evaluate mathematical expressions involving multi-dimensional arrays efficiently.

    - branch/tag used: rel-0.8.2 tag
    - Justification: Stable and well tested
    - Source_Directories:
        - /home/ubuntu/src/theano

- TensorFlow: TensorFlow™ is an open source software library for numerical computation using data flow graphs.

    - branch/tag used : v0.12.1 tag
    - Justification : Stable and well tested
    - Source_Directories :
        - For Python2.7+ - /home/ubuntu/src/tensorflow

- For Python3+ - /home/ubuntu/src/tensorflow3

- For Anaconda Python2.7+ - /home/ubuntu/src/tensorflow_anaconda

- For Anaconda Python3+ - /home/ubuntu/src/tensorflow_anaconda3

- Torch: Torch is a scientific computing framework with wide support for machine learning algorithms that puts GPUs first. It is easy to use and efficient, thanks to an easy and fast scripting language, LuaJIT, and an underlying C/CUDA implementation.

  - branch/tag used : master branch

  - Justification : No other stable branch or tag available

  - Source_Directories :

    - /home/ubuntu/src/torch

- CNTK: CNTK - Microsoft Cognitive Toolkit - is a unified deep-learning toolkit by Microsoft Research.

  - branch/tag used : v2.0beta7.0 tag

  - Justification : Latest release

  - Source_Directories :

    - /home/ubuntu/src/cntk

Python 2.7 and Python 3.5 Support

Python 2.7 and Python 3.5 are supported in the AMI for the following Deep Learning Frameworks:

1. Caffe

2. Tensorflow

3. Theano

4. MXNet

5. CNTK

CPU Instance Type Support

The AMI supports CPU Instance Types for all frameworks. MXNet is built with support for Intel MKL2017 DNN library support. If you want to use the caffe binary for the CPU instance, then you should use the binary inside /home/ubuntu/src/caffe_cpu/

CNTK Python Support

You can run CNTK for Python inside a conda environment. To do this:

```
1 cd /home/ubuntu/src/anaconda3/bin
2     source activate cntk-py34
```

166

GPU Drivers Installed

- CuDNN 5.1
- NVIDIA 352.99
- CUDA 7.5

Launching Deep Learning Instance

Choose the flavor of the AMI from the list below in the region of your choice and follow the steps at:

EC2 Documentation to launch G2 Instance

Testing the Frameworks

The Deep Learning frameworks have been tested with MNIST data. The AMI contains scripts to train and test with MNIST for each of the frameworks. The test checks if the validation accuracy is above a specific threshold. The threshold is different for each of the frameworks.

The scripts are available in the /home/ec2-user/src/bin directory.

The following scripts test the various frameworks:

/home/ubuntu/src/bin/testAll : tests all frameworks

/home/ubuntu/src/bin/testMXNet : tests MXNet

/home/ubuntu/src/bin/testTheano : tests Theano

/home/ubuntu/src/bin/testTensorFlow : tests TensorFlow

/home/ubuntu/src/bin/testTorch : tests Torch

/home/ubuntu/src/bin/testCNTK : tests CNTK

The following tests have been run against each of the frameworks:

- MXNet: This example inside the MXNet repository. Validation accuracy threshold tested for is 97%.
- Tensorflow: This example inside the keras repository. Validation accuracy threshold tested for is 95%.
- Theano: The same example above. Validation accuracy threshold is 95%.
- Torch: This example inside the Torch tree. Validation accuracy threshold is 93%.
- Caffe: This example inside the Caffe repository. Validation accuracy threshold is 98%.
- CNTK: This example inside the CNTK repository. Validation accuracy threshold is 97%.

Ubuntu AMI

Ubuntu based Deep Learning AMIs are available in the following regions:

- eu-west-1(DUB)
- us-east-1(IAD)
- us-west-1(PDX)

References

MXNet

Caffe

Theano

TensorFlow

Torch

CNTK

Test Environments

- Built and Tested on g2.2xlarge.
- Also tested on g2.8xlarge, p2.16xlarge, c4.4xlarge.

Amazon Linux DLAMI Release Archive

- Deep Learning AMI with Source Code (CUDA 9, Amazon Linux) Version: 2.0
- Deep Learning AMI Amazon Linux Version: 3.3_Oct2017
- Deep Learning CUDA 9 AMI Amazon Linux Version: 1.0
- Deep Learning AMI Amazon Linux Version: 3.1_Sep2017
- Deep Learning AMI Amazon Linux Version: 2.3_June2017
- Deep Learning AMI Amazon Linux Version: 2.2_June2017
- Deep Learning AMI Amazon Linux Version: 2.1_Apr2017
- Deep Learning AMI Amazon Linux Version: 2.0
- Deep Learning AMI Amazon Linux Version: 1.5

Deep Learning AMI with Source Code (CUDA 9, Amazon Linux) Version: 2.0

Deep Learning Amazon Machine Image

The Deep Learning AMIs are prebuilt with CUDA9 and MXNet and also contain the Anaconda Platform (Python2 and Python3).

Highlights of the Release

1. Used Deep Learning Base AMI (Amazon Linux) as the base AMI
2. Refreshed TensorFlow master with CUDA9/Volta support
3. MXNet upgraded to v1.0
4. Upgraded PyTorch to v0.3.0
5. Added Keras 2.0.9 support with TensorFlow as the default backend

Prebuilt Deep Learning Frameworks

- Apache MXNet: MXNet is a flexible, efficient, portable and scalable open source library for deep learning. It supports declarative and imperative programming models, across a wide variety of programming languages, making it powerful yet simple to code deep learning applications. MXNet is efficient, inherently supporting automatic parallel scheduling of portions of source code that can be parallelized over a distributed environment. MXNet is also portable, using memory optimizations that allow it to run on mobile phones to full servers.
    - branch/tag used: v1.0
    - Justification: Stable and well tested
    - Source Directories:
        - /home/ec2-user/src/mxnet
- Caffe2: Caffe2 is a cross-platform framework made with expression, speed, and modularity in mind.
    - branch/tag used: v0.8.1 tag
    - Justification: Stable and well tested
    - Note: Available for Python2.7 only
    - Source Directories:
        - For Python2.7+ - /home/ec2-user/src/caffe2
        - For Anaconda Python2.7+ - /home/ec2-user/src/caffe2_anaconda2
- Keras: Keras - Deep Learning Library for Python)

    Tensorflow integration with v2.0.9. Tensorflow is the default backend.
    - Justification : Stable release
    - Source Directories:
        - /home/ec2-user/src/keras

- PyTorch: PyTorch is a python package that provides two high-level features: Tensor computation (like numpy) with strong GPU acceleration, and Deep Neural Networks built on a tape-based autograd system.
    - branch/tag used: v0.3.0
    - Justification: Stable and well tested
    - Source_Directories:
        - /home/ec2-user/src/pytorch
- TensorFlow: TensorFlow™ is an open source software library for numerical computation using data flow graphs.
    - branch/tag used : Master tag
    - Justification : Stable and well tested
    - Source Directories :
        - For Python2.7+ - /home/ec2-user/src/caffe
        - For Python3+ - /home/ec2-user/src/caffe3
        - For Anaconda Python2.7+ - /home/ec2-user/src/caffe_anaconda2
        - For Anaconda3 Python3+ - /home/ec2-user/src/caffe_anaconda3
        - For CPU_ONLY : /home/ec2-user/src/caffe_cpu

Python 2.7 and Python 3.5 Support

Python 2.7 and Python 3.5 are supported in the AMI for the following Deep Learning Frameworks:

1. Apache MXNet
2. Caffe2
3. Keras
4. PyTorch
5. Tensorflow

CPU Instance Type Support

The AMI supports CPU Instance Types for all frameworks. MXNet is built with support for Intel MKL2017 DNN library support.

GPU Drivers Installed

- CuDNN 7
- Nvidia 384.81
- CUDA 9.0

Launching Deep Learning Instance

Choose the flavor of the AMI from the list below in the region of your choice and follow the steps at:

EC2 Documentation to launch P2 Instance

Testing the FrameWorks

The Deep Learning frameworks have been tested with MNIST data. The AMI contains scripts to train and test with MNIST for each of the frameworks.

The scripts are available in the /home/ec2-user/src/bin directory.

The following scripts test the various frameworks:

/home/ec2-user/src/bin/testMXNet : tests MXNet

/home/ec2-user/src/bin/testTensorFlow : tests TensorFlow

/home/ec2-user/src/bin/testCaffe2 : tests Caffe2

The following tests have been run against each of the frameworks:

- MXNet: This example inside the MXNet repository. Validation accuracy threshold tested for is 97%.

- Tensorflow: This example inside the keras repository. Validation accuracy threshold tested for is 95%.

- Caffe2: Based on this example inside the Caffe2 repository. Validation accuracy threshold is 90%.

AMI Region Availability

Available in the following regions:

Region	Code
US East (Ohio)	ec2-us-east-2
US East (N. Virginia)	ec2-us-east-1
US West (N. California)	ec2-us-west-1
US West (Oregon)	ec2-us-west-2
Beijing (China)	cn-north-1
Asia Pacific (Mumbai)	ec2-ap-south-1
Asia Pacific (Seoul)	ec2-ap-northeast-2
Asia Pacific (Singapore)	ec2-ap-southeast-1
Asia Pacific (Sydney)	ec2-ap-southeast-2
Asia Pacific (Tokyo)	ec2-ap-northeast-1
Canada (Central)	ec2-ca-central-1
EU (Frankfurt)	ec2-eu-central-1
EU (Ireland)	ec2-eu-west-1
EU (London)	ec2-eu-west-2
EU (Paris)	ec2-eu-west-3
SA (Sao Paulo)	ec2-sa-east-1

References

- Apache MXNet
- Caffe2
- CNTK
- Keras
- PyTorch
- TensorFlow

- Theano

Test Environments

- Built on p2.16xlarge.
- Also tested on p2.xlarge, c4.4xlarge.

Known Issues

- **Issue**: NCCL is not fully supported. Attempts to use NCCL with any instances but P3 will lead to a crash.

  Workaround: Do not use NCCL on instances other than P3.

- **Issue**: PyTorch tests are broken. ~/src/bin/testPyTorch - installs test environment that is not compatible with the pytorch 0.3.0

  Workaround: N/A

- **Issue**: Tutorials provided by the framework or third parties may have Python dependencies not installed on the DLAMI.

  Workaround: You will need to install those while in the activated environment with conda or pip.

- **Issue**: Module not found error running Caffe2 examples.

  Workaround: Caffe2 optional dependencies are needed for some tutorials

- **Issue**: Caffe2 model download features result in 404. The models have changed locations since the v0.8.1 release. Update models/download.py to use the update from master.

- **Issue**: matplotlib can only render png.

  Workaround: Install Pillow then restart your kernel.

- **Issue**: Changing Caffe2 source code doesn't seem to work.

  Workaround: Change your PYTHONPATH to use the install location `/usr/local/caffe2` instead of the build folder.

- **Issue**: Caffe2 net_drawer errors.

  Workaround: Use the logger patch found in this commit.

- **Issue**: Caffe2 example shows an error regarding LMDB (can't open DB, etc.)

  Workaround: This will require a build from source after installing system LMDB, such as: `sudo apt-get install liblmdb-dev`

- **Issue**: SSH disconnects while using Jupyter server ties up your local port. When trying create a tunnel to the server you see `channel_setup_fwd_listener_tcpip: cannot listen to port: 8057`.

  Workaround: Use `lsof -ti:8057 | xargs kill -9` where 8057 is the local port you used. Then try to create the tunnel to your Jupyter server again.

Deep Learning AMI Amazon Linux Version: 3.3_Oct2017

Deep Learning Amazon Machine Image

The Deep Learning AMIs are pre-built with popular Deep Learning frameworks and also contain the Anaconda Platform (Python2 and Python3).

Highlights of the Release

1. The Linux AMI is now build with 2017.09 base Amazon Linux AMI

2. CUDA 8 support

3. Framework upgrades for Tensorflow(v1.3.0), Caffe2(v0.8.0), Caffe(1.0), CNTK(v2.0), Theano(rel-0.9.0)

Pre-built Deep Learning Frameworks

- MXNet: MXNet is a flexible, efficient, portable and scalable open source library for deep learning. It supports declarative and imperative programming models, across a wide variety of programming languages, making it powerful yet simple to code deep learning applications. MXNet is efficient, inherently supporting automatic parallel scheduling of portions of source code that can be parallelized over a distributed environment. MXNet is also portable, using memory optimizations that allow it to run on mobile phones to full servers.

  - branch/tag used: v0.11.0 tag
  - Justification: Stable and well tested
  - Source_Directories:
    - /home/ec2-user/src/mxnet

- Caffe: Caffe is a deep learning framework made with expression, speed, and modularity in mind. It is developed by the Berkeley Vision and Learning Center (BVLC) and by community contributors.

  - branch/tag used: 1.0 tag
  - Justification: Supports cuda8.0 and cudnn 5.1
  - Source_Directories:
    - For Python2.7+ - /home/ec2-user/src/caffe
    - For Python3+ - /home/ec2-user/src/caffe3
    - For Anaconda Python2.7+ - /home/ec2-user/src/caffe_anaconda2
    - For Anaconda3 Python3+ - /home/ec2-user/src/caffe_anaconda3
    - For CPU_ONLY : /home/ec2-user/src/caffe_cpu

- Caffe2: Caffe2 is a cross-platform framework made with expression, speed, and modularity in mind.

  - branch/tag used: v0.8.0 tag
  - Justification: Stable and well tested
  - Note: Available for Python2.7 only
  - Source_Directories:
    - For Python2.7+ - /home/ec2-user/src/caffe2

- For Anaconda Python2.7+ - /home/ec2-user/src/caffe2_anaconda2
- Theano: Theano is a Python library that allows you to define, optimize, and evaluate mathematical expressions involving multi-dimensional arrays efficiently.
  - branch/tag used: rel-0.9.0 tag
  - Justification: Stable and well tested
  - Source_Directories:
    - /home/ec2-user/src/Theano
- TensorFlow: TensorFlow™ is an open source software library for numerical computation using data flow graphs.
  - branch/tag used : v1.3.0 tag
  - Justification : Stable and well tested
  - Source_Directories :
    - For Python2.7+ - /home/ec2-user/src/tensorflow
    - For Python3+ - /home/ec2-user/src/tensorflow3
    - For Anaconda Python2.7+ - /home/ec2-user/src/tensorflow_anaconda
    - For Anaconda Python3+ - /home/ec2-user/src/tensorflow_anaconda3
- Torch: Torch is a scientific computing framework with wide support for machine learning algorithms that puts GPUs first. It is easy to use and efficient, thanks to an easy and fast scripting language, LuaJIT, and an underlying C/CUDA implementation.
  - branch/tag used : master branch
  - Justification : No other stable branch or tag available
  - Source_Directories :
    - /home/ec2-user/src/torch
- CNTK: CNTK - Microsoft Cognitive Toolkit - is a unified deep-learning toolkit by Microsoft Research.
  - branch/tag used : v2.0 tag
  - Justification : Latest release
  - Source_Directories :
    - /home/ec2-user/src/cntk
- Keras: Keras - Deep Learning Library for Python)
  - branch/tag used : v2.0.8
  - Justification : Stable release
  - Source_Directories:
    - /home/ec2-user/src/keras

Python 2.7 and Python 3.4 Support

Python 2.7 and Python 3.4 are supported in the AMI for the following Deep Learning Frameworks:

1. Caffe
2. Tensorflow

3. Theano

4. MXNet

5. CNTK

CPU Instance Type Support

The AMI supports CPU Instance Types for all frameworks. MXNet is built with support for Intel MKL2017 DNN library support. If you want to use the caffe binary for the CPU instance, then you should use the binary inside /home/ec2-user/src/caffe_cpu/

CNTK Python Support

You can run CNTK for Python inside a conda environment. To do this:

```
1 cd /home/ec2-user/src/anaconda3/bin
2 source activate cntk-py34
```

GPU Drivers Installed

- CuDNN 5.1

- NVIDIA 375.66

- CUDA 8.0

Launching Deep Learning Instance

Choose the flavor of the AMI from the list below in the region of your choice and follow the steps at:

EC2 Documentation to launch P2 Instance

Testing the Frameworks

The Deep Learning frameworks have been tested with MNIST data. The AMI contains scripts to train and test with MNIST for each of the frameworks. The test checks if the validation accuracy is above a specific threshold. The threshold is different for each of the frameworks.

The scripts are available in the /home/ec2-user/src/bin directory.

The following scripts test the various frameworks:

/home/ec2-user/src/bin/testAll : tests all frameworks

/home/ec2-user/src/bin/testMXNet : tests MXNet

/home/ec2-user/src/bin/testTheano : tests Theano

/home/ec2-user/src/bin/testTensorFlow : tests TensorFlow

/home/ec2-user/src/bin/testTorch : tests Torch

/home/ec2-user/src/bin/testCNTK : tests CNTK

/home/ec2-user/src/bin/testCaffe2 : tests Caffe2

The following tests have been run against each of the frameworks:

- MXNet: This example inside the MXNet repository. Validation accuracy threshold tested for is 97%.

- Tensorflow: This example inside the keras repository. Validation accuracy threshold tested for is 95%.

- Theano: The same example above. Validation accuracy threshold is 95%.

- Torch: This example inside the Torch tree. Validation accuracy threshold is 93%.

- Caffe: This example inside the Caffe repository. Validation accuracy threshold is 98%.

- CNTK: This example inside the CNTK repository. Validation accuracy threshold is 97%.

- Caffe2: Based on this example inside the Caffe2 repository. Validation accuracy threshold is 90%.

Amazon Linux AMI

Amazon Linux based Deep Learning AMIs are available in the following regions:

Region	Code
US East (Ohio)	ec2-us-east-2
US East (N. Virginia)	ec2-us-east-1
US West (N. California)	ec2-us-west-1
US West (Oregon)	ec2-us-west-2
Beijing (China)	cn-north-1
Asia Pacific (Mumbai)	ec2-ap-south-1
Asia Pacific (Seoul)	ec2-ap-northeast-2
Asia Pacific (Singapore)	ec2-ap-southeast-1
Asia Pacific (Sydney)	ec2-ap-southeast-2
Asia Pacific (Tokyo)	ec2-ap-northeast-1
Canada (Central)	ec2-ca-central-1
EU (Frankfurt)	ec2-eu-central-1
EU (Ireland)	ec2-eu-west-1
EU (London)	ec2-eu-west-2
EU (Paris)	ec2-eu-west-3
SA (Sao Paulo)	ec2-sa-east-1

References

MXNet

Caffe

Theano

TensorFlow

Torch

CNTK

Test Environments

- Built on p2.16xlarge.

- Also tested on p2.xlarge, p2.8xlarge, p2.16xlarge, c4.4xlarge.

Known Issues

- Need to use sudo to run the testCNTK script.

  e.g.. sudo ./testCNTK

- The conda environments keras1.2_p3 and keras1.2_p2 come with CPU only version of MXNet.

  To use Keras with an MXNet backend to train on GPUs, you can workaround this issue by running the following:

```
1 pip install mxnet-cu80
```

  from inside the conda environment.

Not Supported

- Functioning of multiple frameworks together in the same Python process has not been tested.

  For example, a code snippet like the following:

```
1 import mxnet as mx
2 import tensorflow as tf
```

  in the same Python process may cause an issue.

Deep Learning CUDA 9 AMI Amazon Linux Version: 1.0

Deep Learning Amazon Machine Image

The Deep Learning AMIs are prebuilt with CUDA9 and MXNet and also contain the Anaconda Platform(Python2 and Python3).

Highlights of the Release

1. Used Amazon Linux 2017.09 (ami-8c1be5f6) as the base AMI
2. CUDA 9
3. CuDNN 7
4. NCCL 2.0
5. CUDA 9 support
6. MXNet with CUDA9 Support

Prebuilt Deep Learning Frameworks

- MXNet: MXNet is a flexible, efficient, portable and scalable open source library for deep learning. It supports declarative and imperative programming models, across a wide variety of programming languages, making it powerful yet simple to code deep learning applications. MXNet is efficient, inherently supporting automatic parallel scheduling of portions of source code that can be parallelized over a distributed environment. MXNet is also portable, using memory optimizations that allow it to run on mobile phones to full servers.
  - branch/tag used: v0.12.0 Release Candidate tag
  - Justification: Stable and well tested
  - Source_Directories:
    - /home/ec2-user/src/mxnet
- Caffe2: Caffe2 is a cross-platform framework made with expression, speed, and modularity in mind.
  - branch/tag used: v0.8.1 tag
  - Justification: Stable and well tested
  - Note: Available for Python2.7 only
  - Source_Directories:
    - For Python2.7+ - /home/ec2-user/src/caffe2
    - For Anaconda Python2.7+ - /home/ec2-user/src/caffe2_anaconda2
- TensorFlow: TensorFlow™ is an open source software library for numerical computation using data flow graphs.
  - branch/tag used : Master tag
  - Justification : Stable and well tested
  - Source_Directories :
    - For Python2.7+ - /home/ec2-user/src/tensorflow

- For Python3+ - /home/ec2-user/src/tensorflow3
- For Anaconda Python2.7+ - /home/ec2-user/src/tensorflow_anaconda
- For Anaconda Python3+ - /home/ec2-user/src/tensorflow_anaconda3

Python 2.7 and Python 3.5 Support

Python 2.7 and Python 3.5 are supported in the AMI for the following Deep Learning Frameworks:

1. MXNet
2. Caffe2
3. Tensorflow

CPU Instance Type Support

The AMI supports CPU Instance Types for all frameworks. MXNet is built with support for Intel MKL2017 DNN library support.

GPU Drivers Installed

- CuDNN 7
- Nvidia 384.81
- CUDA 9.0

Launching Deep Learning Instance

Choose the flavor of the AMI from the list below in the region of your choice and follow the steps at:

EC2 Documentation to launch P2 Instance

Testing the FrameWorks

The Deep Learning frameworks have been tested with MNIST data. The AMI contains scripts to train and test with MNIST for each of the frameworks.

The scripts are available in the /home/ec2-user/src/bin directory.

The following scripts test the various frameworks:

/home/ec2-user/src/bin/testMXNet : tests MXNet

/home/ec2-user/src/bin/testTensorFlow : tests TensorFlow

/home/ec2-user/src/bin/testCaffe2 : tests Caffe2

The following tests have been run against each of the frameworks:

- MXNet: This example inside the MXNet repository. Validation accuracy threshold tested for is 97%.
- Tensorflow: This example inside the keras repository. Validation accuracy threshold tested for is 95%.
- Caffe2: Based on this example inside the Caffe2 repository. Validation accuracy threshold is 90%.

Amazon Linux AMI

Amazon Linux based Deep Learning AMIs are available in the following regions:

- eu-west-1(DUB)
- us-east-1(IAD)
- us-west-1(PDX)
- us-east-2(CHM)
- ap-southeast-2(SYD)
- ap-northeast-1(NRT)
- ap-northeast-2(ICN)

References

MXNet

Test Environments

- Built on p2.16xlarge.
- Also tested on p2.xlarge, c4.4xlarge.

Known Issues

- **Issue**: Versions of pip and Python are not compatible for the Amazon Linux Deep Learning AMI (DLAMI), specifically pip, which is expected to install Python 2 bindings, but instead installs Python 3 bindings.

  This is a known problem documented on the pip website. A future release will address this issue.

  Workaround: Use the relevant command below to install the package for the appropriate Python version:

  python2.7 -m pip install *some-python-package*

  python3.4 -m pip install *some-python-package*

- **Issue**: Tutorials provided by the framework or third parties may have Python dependencies not installed on the DLAMI.

  Workaround: You will need to install those while in the activated environment with conda or pip.

- **Issue**: Module not found error running Caffe2 examples.

  Workaround: Caffe2 optional dependencies are needed for some tutorials

- **Issue**: Caffe2 model download features result in 404. The models have changed locations since the v0.8.1 release. Update models/download.py to use the update from master.

- **Issue**: matplotlib can only render png.

  Workaround: Install Pillow then restart your kernel.

- **Issue**: Changing Caffe2 source code doesn't seem to work.

  Workaround: Change your PYTHONPATH to use the install location `/usr/local/caffe2` instead of the build folder.

- **Issue**: Caffe2 net_drawer errors.

  Workaround: Use the logger patch found in this commit.

- **Issue**: Caffe2 example shows an error regarding LMDB (can't open DB, etc.)

  Workaround: This will require a build from source after installing system LMDB, such as: `sudo apt-get install liblmdb-dev`

- **Issue**: SSH disconnects while using Jupyter server ties up your local port. When trying create a tunnel to the server you see `channel_setup_fwd_listener_tcpip: cannot listen to port: 8157`.

  Workaround: Use `lsof -ti:8057 | xargs kill -9` where 8057 is the local port you used. Then try to create the tunnel to your Jupyter server again.

Deep Learning AMI Amazon Linux Version: 3.1_Sep2017

Deep Learning Amazon Machine Image

The Deep Learning AMIs are pre-built with popular Deep Learning frameworks and also contain the Anaconda Platform (Python2 and Python3).

Highlights of the Release

1. CUDA 8 support
2. Framework upgrades for Tensorflow(v1.3.0), Caffe2(v0.8.0), Caffe(1.0), CNTK(v2.0), Theano(rel-0.9.0)

Pre-built Deep Learning Frameworks

- MXNet: MXNet is a flexible, efficient, portable and scalable open source library for deep learning. It supports declarative and imperative programming models, across a wide variety of programming languages, making it powerful yet simple to code deep learning applications. MXNet is efficient, inherently supporting automatic parallel scheduling of portions of source code that can be parallelized over a distributed environment. MXNet is also portable, using memory optimizations that allow it to run on mobile phones to full servers.
  - branch/tag used: v0.11.0 tag
  - Justification: Stable and well tested
  - Source_Directories:
    - /home/ec2-user/src/mxnet
- Caffe: Caffe is a deep learning framework made with expression, speed, and modularity in mind. It is developed by the Berkeley Vision and Learning Center (BVLC) and by community contributors.
  - branch/tag used: 1.0 tag
  - Justification: Supports cuda8.0 and cudnn 5.1
  - Source_Directories:
    - For Python2.7+ - /home/ec2-user/src/caffe
    - For Python3+ - /home/ec2-user/src/caffe3
    - For Anaconda Python2.7+ - /home/ec2-user/src/caffe_anaconda2
    - For Anaconda3 Python3+ - /home/ec2-user/src/caffe_anaconda3
    - For CPU_ONLY : /home/ec2-user/src/caffe_cpu
- Caffe2: Caffe2 is a cross-platform framework made with expression, speed, and modularity in mind.
  - branch/tag used: v0.8.0 tag
  - Justification: Stable and well tested
  - Note: Available for Python2.7 only
  - Source_Directories:
    - For Python2.7+ - /home/ec2-user/src/caffe2
    - For Anaconda Python2.7+ - /home/ec2-user/src/caffe2_anaconda2

- Theano: Theano is a Python library that allows you to define, optimize, and evaluate mathematical expressions involving multi-dimensional arrays efficiently.

  - branch/tag used: rel-0.9.0 tag

  - Justification: Stable and well tested

  - Source_Directories:

    - /home/ec2-user/src/Theano

- TensorFlow: TensorFlow™ is an open source software library for numerical computation using data flow graphs.

  - branch/tag used : v1.3.0 tag

  - Justification : Stable and well tested

  - Source_Directories :

    - For Python2.7+ - /home/ec2-user/src/tensorflow

    - For Python3+ - /home/ec2-user/src/tensorflow3

    - For Anaconda Python2.7+ - /home/ec2-user/src/tensorflow_anaconda

    - For Anaconda Python3+ - /home/ec2-user/src/tensorflow_anaconda3

- Torch: Torch is a scientific computing framework with wide support for machine learning algorithms that puts GPUs first. It is easy to use and efficient, thanks to an easy and fast scripting language, LuaJIT, and an underlying C/CUDA implementation.

  - branch/tag used : master branch

  - Justification : No other stable branch or tag available

  - Source_Directories :

    - /home/ec2-user/src/torch

- CNTK: CNTK - Microsoft Cognitive Toolkit - is a unified deep-learning toolkit by Microsoft Research.

  - branch/tag used : v2.0 tag

  - Justification : Latest release

  - Source_Directories :

    - /home/ec2-user/src/cntk

- Keras: Keras - Deep Learning Library for Python)

  - branch/tag used : master

  - Justification : Stable release (1.2.2 with MXNet support)

  - Source_Directories:

    - /home/ec2-user/src/keras

Python 2.7 and Python 3.5 Support

Python 2.7 and Python 3.5 are supported in the AMI for the following Deep Learning Frameworks:

1. Caffe

2. Tensorflow

3. Theano

4. MXNet

5. CNTK

CPU Instance Type Support

The AMI supports CPU Instance Types for all frameworks. MXNet is built with support for Intel MKL2017 DNN library support. If you want to use the caffe binary for the CPU instance, then you should use the binary inside /home/ec2-user/src/caffe_cpu/

CNTK Python Support

You can run CNTK for Python inside a conda environment. To do this:

```
1  cd /home/ec2-user/src/anaconda3/bin
2        source activate cntk-py34
```

GPU Drivers Installed

- CuDNN 5.1
- NVIDIA 375.66
- CUDA 8.0

Launching Deep Learning Instance

Choose the flavor of the AMI from the list below in the region of your choice and follow the steps at:

EC2 Documentation to launch P2 Instance

Testing the Frameworks

The Deep Learning frameworks have been tested with MNIST data. The AMI contains scripts to train and test with MNIST for each of the frameworks. The test checks if the validation accuracy is above a specific threshold. The threshold is different for each of the frameworks.

The scripts are available in the /home/ec2-user/src/bin directory.

The following scripts test the various frameworks:

/home/ec2-user/src/bin/testAll : tests all frameworks

/home/ec2-user/src/bin/testMXNet : tests MXNet

/home/ec2-user/src/bin/testTheano : tests Theano

/home/ec2-user/src/bin/testTensorFlow : tests TensorFlow

/home/ec2-user/src/bin/testTorch : tests Torch

/home/ec2-user/src/bin/testCNTK : tests CNTK

/home/ec2-user/src/bin/testCaffe2 : tests Caffe2

The following tests have been run against each of the frameworks:

- MXNet: This example inside the MXNet repository. Validation accuracy threshold tested for is 97%.

- Tensorflow: This example inside the keras repository. Validation accuracy threshold tested for is 95%.

- Theano: The same example above. Validation accuracy threshold is 95%.

- Torch: This example inside the Torch tree. Validation accuracy threshold is 93%.

- Caffe: This example inside the Caffe repository. Validation accuracy threshold is 98%.

- CNTK: This example inside the CNTK repository. Validation accuracy threshold is 97%.

- Caffe2: Based on this example inside the Caffe2 repository. Validation accuracy threshold is 90%.

Amazon Linux AMI

Amazon Linux based Deep Learning AMIs are available in the following regions:

- eu-west-1(DUB)
- us-east-1(IAD)
- us-west-1(PDX)
- us-east-2(CHM)
- ap-southeast-2(SYD)
- ap-northeast-1(NRT)
- ap-northeast-2(ICN)

References

MXNet

Caffe

Theano

TensorFlow

Torch

CNTK

Test Environments

- Built on p2.16xlarge.
- Also tested on p2.xlarge, p2.8xlarge, p2.16xlarge, c4.4xlarge.

Known Issues

- Need to use sudo to run the testCNTK script.

  e.g.. sudo ./testCNTK

Not Supported

- Functioning of multiple frameworks together in the same Python process has not been tested.

  For example, a code snippet like the following:

```
1 import mxnet as mx
2          import tensorflow as tf
```

  in the same Python process may cause an issue.

Deep Learning AMI Amazon Linux Version: 2.3_June2017

Deep Learning Amazon Machine Image

The Deep Learning AMIs are pre-built with popular Deep Learning frameworks and also contain the Anaconda Platform (Python2 and Python3).

Highlights of the Release

1. MXNet compiled with S3 Support(USE_S3=1).
2. Security fixes applied for Stackclash security issue. (https://alas.aws.amazon.com/ALAS-2017-845.html)

Pre-built Deep Learning Frameworks

- MXNet: MXNet is a flexible, efficient, portable and scalable open source library for deep learning. It supports declarative and imperative programming models, across a wide variety of programming languages, making it powerful yet simple to code deep learning applications. MXNet is efficient, inherently supporting automatic parallel scheduling of portions of source code that can be parallelized over a distributed environment. MXNet is also portable, using memory optimizations that allow it to run on mobile phones to full servers.
  - branch/tag used: v0.10.0 tag
  - Justification: Stable and well tested
  - Source_Directories:
    - /home/ec2-user/src/mxnet
- Caffe: Caffe is a deep learning framework made with expression, speed, and modularity in mind. It is developed by the Berkeley Vision and Learning Center (BVLC) and by community contributors.
  - branch/tag used: rc5 tag
  - Justification: Supports cuda7.5 and cudnn 5.1
  - Source_Directories:
    - For Python2.7+ - /home/ec2-user/src/caffe
    - For Python3+ - /home/ec2-user/src/caffe3
    - For Anaconda Python2.7+ - /home/ec2-user/src/caffe_anaconda2
    - For Anaconda3 Python3+ - /home/ec2-user/src/caffe_anaconda3
    - For CPU_ONLY : /home/ec2-user/src/caffe_cpu
- Caffe2: Caffe2 is a cross-platform framework made with expression, speed, and modularity in mind.
  - branch/tag used: v0.7.0 tag
  - Justification: Stable and well tested
  - Note: Available for Python2.7 only
  - Source_Directories:
    - For Python2.7+ - /home/ec2-user/src/caffe2
    - For Anaconda Python2.7+ - /home/ec2-user/src/caffe2_anaconda2

- Theano: Theano is a Python library that allows you to define, optimize, and evaluate mathematical expressions involving multi-dimensional arrays efficiently.
  - branch/tag used: rel-0.9.0 tag
  - Justification: Stable and well tested
  - Source_Directories:
    - /home/ec2-user/src/Theano
- TensorFlow: TensorFlow™ is an open source software library for numerical computation using data flow graphs.
  - branch/tag used : v1.1.0 tag
  - Justification : Stable and well tested
  - Source_Directories :
    - For Python2.7+ - /home/ec2-user/src/tensorflow
    - For Python3+ - /home/ec2-user/src/tensorflow3
    - For Anaconda Python2.7+ - /home/ec2-user/src/tensorflow_anaconda
    - For Anaconda Python3+ - /home/ec2-user/src/tensorflow_anaconda3
- Torch: Torch is a scientific computing framework with wide support for machine learning algorithms that puts GPUs first. It is easy to use and efficient, thanks to an easy and fast scripting language, LuaJIT, and an underlying C/CUDA implementation.
  - branch/tag used : master branch
  - Justification : No other stable branch or tag available
  - Source_Directories :
    - /home/ec2-user/src/torch
- CNTK: CNTK - Microsoft Cognitive Toolkit - is a unified deep-learning toolkit by Microsoft Research.
  - branch/tag used : v2.0.rc1 tag
  - Justification : Latest release
  - Source_Directories :
    - /home/ec2-user/src/cntk
- Keras: Keras - Deep Learning Library for Python)
  - branch/tag used : 1.2.2 tag
  - Justification : Stable release
  - Source_Directories:
    - /home/ec2-user/src/keras

Python 2.7 and Python 3.5 Support

Python 2.7 and Python 3.5 are supported in the AMI for the following Deep Learning Frameworks:

1. Caffe
2. Tensorflow
3. Theano

4. MXNet

5. CNTK

CPU Instance Type Support

The AMI supports CPU Instance Types for all frameworks. MXNet is built with support for Intel MKL2017 DNN library support. If you want to use the caffe binary for the CPU instance, then you should use the binary inside /home/ec2-user/src/caffe_cpu/

CNTK Python Support

You can run CNTK for Python inside a conda environment. To do this:

```
1  cd /home/ec2-user/src/anaconda3/bin
2        source activate cntk-py34
```

GPU Drivers Installed

- CuDNN 5.1
- NVIDIA 367.57
- CUDA 7.5

Launching Deep Learning Instance

Choose the flavor of the AMI from the list below in the region of your choice and follow the steps at:

EC2 Documentation to launch G2 Instance

Testing the Frameworks

The Deep Learning frameworks have been tested with MNIST data. The AMI contains scripts to train and test with MNIST for each of the frameworks. The test checks if the validation accuracy is above a specific threshold. The threshold is different for each of the frameworks.

The scripts are available in the /home/ec2-user/src/bin directory.

The following scripts test the various frameworks:

/home/ec2-user/src/bin/testAll : tests all frameworks

/home/ec2-user/src/bin/testMXNet : tests MXNet

/home/ec2-user/src/bin/testTheano : tests Theano

/home/ec2-user/src/bin/testTensorFlow : tests TensorFlow

/home/ec2-user/src/bin/testTorch : tests Torch

/home/ec2-user/src/bin/testCNTK : tests CNTK

/home/ec2-user/src/bin/testCaffe2 : tests Caffe2

The following tests have been run against each of the frameworks:

- MXNet: This example inside the MXNet repository. Validation accuracy threshold tested for is 97%.

- Tensorflow: This example inside the keras repository. Validation accuracy threshold tested for is 95%.

- Theano: The same example above. Validation accuracy threshold is 95%.

- Torch: This example inside the Torch tree. Validation accuracy threshold is 93%.

- Caffe: This example inside the Caffe repository. Validation accuracy threshold is 98%.

- CNTK: This example inside the CNTK repository. Validation accuracy threshold is 97%.

- Caffe2: Based on this example inside the Caffe2 repository. Validation accuracy threshold is 90%.

Amazon Linux AMI

Amazon Linux based Deep Learning AMIs are available in the following regions:

- eu-west-1(DUB)
- us-east-1(IAD)
- us-west-1(PDX)
- us-east-2(CHM)
- ap-southeast-2(SYD)
- ap-northeast-1(NRT)
- ap-northeast-2(ICN)

References

MXNet

Caffe

Theano

TensorFlow

Torch

CNTK

Test Environments

- Built on p2.16xlarge.
- Also tested on g2.2xlarge, g2.8xlarge, p2.xlarge, p2.8xlarge, p2.16xlarge, c4.4xlarge.

Known Issues

- Need to use sudo to run the testCNTK script.

  e.g. sudo ./testCNTK

Not Supported

- Functioning of multiple frameworks together in the same Python process has not been tested. For example, a code snippet like the following:

```
1  import mxnet as mx
2          import tensorflow as tf
```

in the same Python process may cause an issue.

Deep Learning AMI Amazon Linux Version: 2.2_June2017

Deep Learning Amazon Machine Image

The Deep Learning AMIs are pre-built with popular Deep Learning frameworks and also contain the Anaconda Platform (Python2 and Python3).

Pre-built Deep Learning Frameworks

- MXNet: MXNet is a flexible, efficient, portable and scalable open source library for deep learning. It supports declarative and imperative programming models, across a wide variety of programming languages, making it powerful yet simple to code deep learning applications. MXNet is efficient, inherently supporting automatic parallel scheduling of portions of source code that can be parallelized over a distributed environment. MXNet is also portable, using memory optimizations that allow it to run on mobile phones to full servers.
    - branch/tag used: v0.10.0 tag
    - Justification: Stable and well tested
    - Source_Directories:
        - /home/ec2-user/src/mxnet
- Caffe: Caffe is a deep learning framework made with expression, speed, and modularity in mind. It is developed by the Berkeley Vision and Learning Center (BVLC) and by community contributors.
    - branch/tag used: rc5 tag
    - Justification: Supports cuda7.5 and cudnn 5.1
    - Source_Directories:
        - For Python2.7+ - /home/ec2-user/src/caffe
        - For Python3+ - /home/ec2-user/src/caffe3
        - For Anaconda Python2.7+ - /home/ec2-user/src/caffe_anaconda2
        - For Anaconda3 Python3+ - /home/ec2-user/src/caffe_anaconda3
        - For CPU_ONLY : /home/ec2-user/src/caffe_cpu
- Caffe2: Caffe2 is a cross-platform framework made with expression, speed, and modularity in mind.
    - branch/tag used: v0.7.0 tag
    - Justification: Stable and well tested
    - Note: Available for Python2.7 only
    - Source_Directories:
        - For Python2.7+ - /home/ec2-user/src/caffe2
        - For Anaconda Python2.7+ - /home/ec2-user/src/caffe2_anaconda2
- Theano: Theano is a Python library that allows you to define, optimize, and evaluate mathematical expressions involving multi-dimensional arrays efficiently.
    - branch/tag used: rel-0.9.0 tag
    - Justification: Stable and well tested
    - Source_Directories:

- /home/ec2-user/src/Theano

- TensorFlow: TensorFlow™ is an open source software library for numerical computation using data flow graphs.

  - branch/tag used : v1.1.0 tag

  - Justification : Stable and well tested

  - Source_Directories :

    - For Python2.7+ - /home/ec2-user/src/tensorflow

    - For Python3+ - /home/ec2-user/src/tensorflow3

    - For Anaconda Python2.7+ - /home/ec2-user/src/tensorflow_anaconda

    - For Anaconda Python3+ - /home/ec2-user/src/tensorflow_anaconda3

- Torch: Torch is a scientific computing framework with wide support for machine learning algorithms that puts GPUs first. It is easy to use and efficient, thanks to an easy and fast scripting language, LuaJIT, and an underlying C/CUDA implementation.

  - branch/tag used : master branch

  - Justification : No other stable branch or tag available

  - Source_Directories :

    - /home/ec2-user/src/torch

- CNTK: CNTK - Microsoft Cognitive Toolkit - is a unified deep-learning toolkit by Microsoft Research.

  - branch/tag used : v2.0.rc1 tag

  - Justification : Latest release

  - Source_Directories :

    - /home/ec2-user/src/cntk

- Keras: Keras - Deep Learning Library for Python)

  - branch/tag used : 1.2.2 tag

  - Justification : Stable release

  - Source_Directories:

    - /home/ec2-user/src/keras

Python 2.7 and Python 3.5 Support

Python 2.7 and Python 3.5 are supported in the AMI for the following Deep Learning Frameworks:

1. Caffe

2. Tensorflow

3. Theano

4. MXNet

5. CNTK

CPU Instance Type Support

The AMI supports CPU Instance Types for all frameworks. MXNet is built with support for Intel MKL2017 DNN library support. If you want to use the caffe binary for the CPU instance, then you should use the binary inside /home/ec2-user/src/caffe_cpu/

CNTK Python Support

You can run CNTK for Python inside a conda environment. To do this:

```
1 cd /home/ec2-user/src/anaconda3/bin
2        source activate cntk-py34
```

GPU Drivers Installed

- CuDNN 5.1
- NVIDIA 367.57
- CUDA 7.5

Launching Deep Learning Instance

Choose the flavor of the AMI from the list below in the region of your choice and follow the steps at:

EC2 Documentation to launch G2 Instance

Testing the Frameworks

The Deep Learning frameworks have been tested with MNIST data. The AMI contains scripts to train and test with MNIST for each of the frameworks. The test checks if the validation accuracy is above a specific threshold. The threshold is different for each of the frameworks.

The scripts are available in the /home/ec2-user/src/bin directory.

The following scripts test the various frameworks:

/home/ec2-user/src/bin/testAll : tests all frameworks

/home/ec2-user/src/bin/testMXNet : tests MXNet

/home/ec2-user/src/bin/testTheano : tests Theano

/home/ec2-user/src/bin/testTensorFlow : tests TensorFlow

/home/ec2-user/src/bin/testTorch : tests Torch

/home/ec2-user/src/bin/testCNTK : tests CNTK

/home/ec2-user/src/bin/testCaffe2 : tests Caffe2

The following tests have been run against each of the frameworks:

- MXNet: This example inside the MXNet repository. Validation accuracy threshold tested for is 97%.
- Tensorflow: This example inside the keras repository. Validation accuracy threshold tested for is 95%.
- Theano: The same example above. Validation accuracy threshold is 95%.
- Torch: This example inside the Torch tree. Validation accuracy threshold is 93%.

- Caffe: This example inside the Caffe repository. Validation accuracy threshold is 98%.
- CNTK: This example inside the CNTK repository. Validation accuracy threshold is 97%.
- Caffe2: Based on this example inside the Caffe2 repository. Validation accuracy threshold is 90%.

Amazon Linux AMI

Amazon Linux based Deep Learning AMIs are available in the following regions:

- eu-west-1(DUB)
- us-east-1(IAD)
- us-west-1(PDX)
- us-east-2(CHM)
- ap-southeast-2(SYD)
- ap-northeast-1(NRT)
- ap-northeast-2(ICN)

References

MXNet

Caffe

Theano

TensorFlow

Torch

CNTK

Test Environments

- Built and Tested on g2.2xlarge.
- Also tested on g2.8xlarge, p2.16xlarge, c4.4xlarge.

Known Issues

- Need to use sudo to run the testCNTK script.

  e.g. sudo ./testCNTK

Not Supported

- Functioning of multiple frameworks together in the same Python process has not been tested.

  For example, a code snippet like the following:

```
1 import mxnet as mx
2         import tensorflow as tf
```

  in the same Python process may cause an issue.

Deep Learning AMI Amazon Linux Version: 2.1_Apr2017

Deep Learning Amazon Machine Image

The Deep Learning AMIs are pre-built with popular Deep Learning frameworks and also contain the Anaconda Platform(Python2 and Python3).

Pre-built Deep Learning Frameworks

- MXNet: MXNet is a flexible, efficient, portable and scalable open source library for deep learning. It supports declarative and imperative programming models, across a wide variety of programming languages, making it powerful yet simple to code deep learning applications. MXNet is efficient, inherently supporting automatic parallel scheduling of portions of source code that can be parallelized over a distributed environment. MXNet is also portable, using memory optimizations that allow it to run on mobile phones to full servers.

  - branch/tag used: v0.9.3 tag
  - Justification: Stable and well tested
  - Source_Directories:
    - /home/ec2-user/src/mxnet

- Caffe: Caffe is a deep learning framework made with expression, speed, and modularity in mind. It is developed by the Berkeley Vision and Learning Center (BVLC) and by community contributors.

  - branch/tag used: rc5 tag
  - Justification: Supports cuda7.5 and cudnn 5.1
  - Source_Directories:
    - For Python2.7+ - /home/ec2-user/src/caffe
    - For Python3+ - /home/ec2-user/src/caffe3
    - For Anaconda Python2.7+ - /home/ec2-user/src/caffe_anaconda2
    - For Anaconda3 Python3+ - /home/ec2-user/src/caffe_anaconda3
    - For CPU_ONLY : /home/ec2-user/src/caffe_cpu

- Caffe2: Caffe2 is a cross-platform framework made with expression, speed, and modularity in mind.

  - branch/tag used: v0.7.0 tag
  - Justification: Stable and well tested
  - Note: Available for Python2.7 only
  - Source_Directories:
    - For Python2.7+ - /home/ec2-user/src/caffe2
    - For Anaconda Python2.7+ - /home/ec2-user/src/caffe2_anaconda2

- Theano: Theano is a Python library that allows you to define, optimize, and evaluate mathematical expressions involving multi-dimensional arrays efficiently.

  - branch/tag used: rel-0.8.2 tag
  - Justification: Stable and well tested
  - Source_Directories:

- /home/ec2-user/src/Theano
- TensorFlow: TensorFlow™ is an open source software library for numerical computation using data flow graphs.
  - branch/tag used : v1.0.1 tag
  - Justification : Stable and well tested
  - Source_Directories :
    - For Python2.7+ - /home/ec2-user/src/tensorflow
    - For Python3+ - /home/ec2-user/src/tensorflow3
    - For Anaconda Python2.7+ - /home/ec2-user/src/tensorflow_anaconda
    - For Anaconda Python3+ - /home/ec2-user/src/tensorflow_anaconda3
- Torch: Torch is a scientific computing framework with wide support for machine learning algorithms that puts GPUs first. It is easy to use and efficient, thanks to an easy and fast scripting language, LuaJIT, and an underlying C/CUDA implementation.
  - branch/tag used : master branch
  - Justification : No other stable branch or tag available
  - Source_Directories :
    - /home/ec2-user/src/torch
- CNTK: CNTK - Microsoft Cognitive Toolkit - is a unified deep-learning toolkit by Microsoft Research.
  - branch/tag used : v2.0.rc1 tag
  - Justification : Latest release
  - Source_Directories :
    - /home/ec2-user/src/cntk
- Keras: Keras - Deep Learning Library for Python)
  - branch/tag used : 1.2.2 tag
  - Justification : Stable release
  - Source_Directories:
    - /home/ec2-user/src/keras

Python 2.7 and Python3.5 Support

Python2.7 and Python3.5 are supported in the AMI for the following Deep Learning Frameworks:

1. Caffe
2. Tensorflow
3. Theano
4. MXNet
5. CNTK

CPU Instance Type Support

The AMI supports CPU Instance Types for all frameworks. MXNet is built with support for Intel MKL2017 DNN library support. If you want to use the caffe binary for the CPU instance, then you should use the binary inside /home/ec2-user/src/caffe_cpu/

CNTK Python Support

You can run CNTK for Python inside a conda environment. To do this:

```
1 cd /home/ec2-user/src/anaconda3/bin
2        source activate cntk-py34
```

GPU Drivers Installed

- CuDNN 5.1
- NVIDIA 367.57
- CUDA 7.5

Launching Deep Learning Instance

Choose the flavor of the AMI from the list below in the region of your choice and follow the steps at:

EC2 Documentation to launch G2 Instance

Testing the Frameworks

The Deep Learning frameworks have been tested with MNIST data. The AMI contains scripts to train and test with MNIST for each of the frameworks. The test checks if the validation accuracy is above a specific threshold. The threshold is different for each of the frameworks.

The scripts are available in the /home/ec2-user/src/bin directory.

The following scripts test the various frameworks:

/home/ec2-user/src/bin/testAll : tests all frameworks

/home/ec2-user/src/bin/testMXNet : tests MXNet

/home/ec2-user/src/bin/testTheano : tests Theano

/home/ec2-user/src/bin/testTensorFlow : tests TensorFlow

/home/ec2-user/src/bin/testTorch : tests Torch

/home/ec2-user/src/bin/testCNTK : tests CNTK

/home/ec2-user/src/bin/testCaffe2 : tests Caffe2

The following tests have been run against each of the frameworks:

- MXNet: This example inside the MXNet repository. Validation accuracy threshold tested for is 97%.
- Tensorflow: This example inside the keras repository. Validation accuracy threshold tested for is 95%.
- Theano: The same example above. Validation accuracy threshold is 95%.
- Torch: This example inside the Torch tree. Validation accuracy threshold is 93%.

- Caffe: This example inside the Caffe repository. Validation accuracy threshold is 98%.
- CNTK: This example inside the CNTK repository. Validation accuracy threshold is 97%.
- Caffe2: Based on this example inside the Caffe2 repository. Validation accuracy threshold is 90%.

Amazon Linux AMI

Amazon Linux based Deep Learning AMIs are available in the following regions:
- eu-west-1(DUB)
- us-east-1(IAD)
- us-west-1(PDX)

References

MXNet

Caffe

Theano

TensorFlow

Torch

CNTK

Test Environments

- Built and Tested on g2.2xlarge.
- Also tested on g2.8xlarge, p2.16xlarge, c4.4xlarge.

Known Issues

- Need to use sudo to run the testCNTK script.

  e.g. sudo ./testCNTK

Not Supported

- Functioning of multiple frameworks together in the same Python process has not been tested.

  For example, a code snippet like the following:

```
1 import mxnet as mx
2         import tensorflow as tf
```

in the same Python process may cause an issue.

Deep Learning AMI Amazon Linux Version: 2.0

Deep Learning Amazon Machine Image

The Deep Learning AMIs are pre-built with popular Deep Learning frameworks and also contain the Anaconda Platform (Python2 and Python3).

Pre-built Deep Learning Frameworks

- MXNet: MXNet is a flexible, efficient, portable and scalable open source library for deep learning. It supports declarative and imperative programming models, across a wide variety of programming languages, making it powerful yet simple to code deep learning applications. MXNet is efficient, inherently supporting automatic parallel scheduling of portions of source code that can be parallelized over a distributed environment. MXNet is also portable, using memory optimizations that allow it to run on mobile phones to full servers.
  - branch/tag used: v0.9.3 tag
  - Justification: Stable and well tested
  - Source_Directories:
    - /home/ec2-user/src/mxnet
- Caffe: Caffe is a deep learning framework made with expression, speed, and modularity in mind. It is developed by the Berkeley Vision and Learning Center (BVLC) and by community contributors.
  - branch/tag used: rc5 tag
  - Justification: Supports cuda7.5 and cudnn 5.1
  - Source_Directories:
    - For Python2.7+ - /home/ec2-user/src/caffe
    - For Python3+ - /home/ec2-user/src/caffe3
    - For Anaconda Python2.7+ - /home/ec2-user/src/caffe_anaconda2
    - For Anaconda3 Python3+ - /home/ec2-user/src/caffe_anaconda3
    - For CPU_ONLY : /home/ec2-user/src/caffe_cpu
- Theano: Theano is a Python library that allows you to define, optimize, and evaluate mathematical expressions involving multi-dimensional arrays efficiently.
  - branch/tag used: rel-0.8.2 tag
  - Justification: Stable and well tested
  - Source_Directories:
    - /home/ec2-user/src/Theano
- TensorFlow: TensorFlow™ is an open source software library for numerical computation using data flow graphs.
  - branch/tag used : v1.0.0 tag
  - Justification : Stable and well tested
  - Source_Directories :
    - For Python2.7+ - /home/ec2-user/src/tensorflow

- For Python3+ - /home/ec2-user/src/tensorflow3
- For Anaconda Python2.7+ - /home/ec2-user/src/tensorflow_anaconda
- For Anaconda Python3+ - /home/ec2-user/src/tensorflow_anaconda3

- Torch: Torch is a scientific computing framework with wide support for machine learning algorithms that puts GPUs first. It is easy to use and efficient, thanks to an easy and fast scripting language, LuaJIT, and an underlying C/CUDA implementation.
  - branch/tag used : master branch
  - Justification : No other stable branch or tag available
  - Source_Directories :
    - /home/ec2-user/src/torch

- CNTK: CNTK - Microsoft Cognitive Toolkit - is a unified deep-learning toolkit by Microsoft Research.
  - branch/tag used : v2.0beta12.0 tag
  - Justification : Latest release
  - Source Directories :
    - /home/ec2-user/src/cntk

- Keras: Keras - Deep Learning Library for Python)
  - branch/tag used : 1.2.2 tag
  - Justification : Stable release
  - Source_Directories:
    - /home/ec2-user/src/keras

Python 2.7 and Python 3.5 Support

Python 2.7 and Python 3.5 are supported in the AMI for the following Deep Learning Frameworks:

1. Caffe
2. Tensorflow
3. Theano
4. MXNet
5. CNTK

CPU Instance Type Support

The AMI supports CPU Instance Types for all frameworks. MXNet is built with support for Intel MKL2017 DNN library support. If you want to use the caffe binary for the CPU instance, then you should use the binary inside /home/ec2-user/src/caffe_cpu/

CNTK Python Support

You can run CNTK for Python inside a conda environment. To do this:

```
1 cd /home/ec2-user/src/anaconda3/bin
2         source activate cntk-py34
```

GPU Drivers Installed

- CuDNN 5.1
- NVIDIA 367.57
- CUDA 7.5

Launching Deep Learning Instance

Choose the flavor of the AMI from the list below in the region of your choice and follow the steps at:

EC2 Documentation to launch G2 Instance

Testing the Frameworks

The Deep Learning frameworks have been tested with MNIST data. The AMI contains scripts to train and test with MNIST for each of the frameworks. The test checks if the validation accuracy is above a specific threshold. The threshold is different for each of the frameworks.

The scripts are available in the /home/ec2-user/src/bin directory.

The following scripts test the various frameworks:

/home/ec2-user/src/bin/testAll : tests all frameworks

/home/ec2-user/src/bin/testMXNet : tests MXNet

/home/ec2-user/src/bin/testTheano : tests Theano

/home/ec2-user/src/bin/testTensorFlow : tests TensorFlow

/home/ec2-user/src/bin/testTorch : tests Torch

/home/ec2-user/src/bin/testCNTK : tests CNTK

The following tests have been run against each of the frameworks:

- MXNet: This example inside the MXNet repository. Validation accuracy threshold tested for is 97%.
- Tensorflow: This example inside the keras repository. Validation accuracy threshold tested for is 95%.
- Theano: The same example above. Validation accuracy threshold is 95%.
- Torch: This example inside the Torch tree. Validation accuracy threshold is 93%.
- Caffe: This example inside the Caffe repository. Validation accuracy threshold is 98%.
- CNTK: This example inside the CNTK repository. Validation accuracy threshold is 97%.

Amazon Linux AMI

Amazon Linux based Deep Learning AMIs are available in the following regions:

- eu-west-1(DUB)
- us-east-1(IAD)
- us-west-1(PDX)

References

MXNet

Caffe

Theano

TensorFlow

Torch

CNTK

Test Environments

- Built and Tested on g2.2xlarge.
- Also tested on g2.8xlarge, p2.16xlarge, c4.4xlarge.

Known Issues

- Need to use sudo to run the testCNTK script.

  e.g. sudo ./testCNTK

Not Supported

- Functioning of multiple frameworks together in the same Python process has not been tested.

  For example, a code snippet like the following:

```
1 import mxnet as mx
2         import tensorflow as tf
```

Deep Learning AMI Amazon Linux Version: 1.5

Deep Learning Amazon Machine Image

The Deep Learning AMIs are pre-built with popular Deep Learning frameworks and also contain the Anaconda Platform(Python2 and Python3).

Pre-built Deep Learning Frameworks

- MXNet: MXNet is a flexible, efficient, portable and scalable open source library for deep learning. It supports declarative and imperative programming models, across a wide variety of programming languages, making it powerful yet simple to code deep learning applications. MXNet is efficient, inherently supporting automatic parallel scheduling of portions of source code that can be parallelized over a distributed environment. MXNet is also portable, using memory optimizations that allow it to run on mobile phones to full servers.
    - branch/tag used: master branch
    - Justification: Stable and well tested
    - Source_Directories:
        - /home/ec2-user/src/mxnet
- Caffe: Caffe is a deep learning framework made with expression, speed, and modularity in mind. It is developed by the Berkeley Vision and Learning Center (BVLC) and by community contributors.
    - branch/tag used: master branch
    - Justification: Supports cuda7.5 and cudnn 5.1
    - Source_Directories:
        - For Python2.7+ - /home/ec2-user/src/caffe
        - For Python3+ - /home/ec2-user/src/caffe3
        - For Python3+ - /home/ec2-user/src/caffe3
- Theano: Theano is a Python library that allows you to define, optimize, and evaluate mathematical expressions involving multi-dimensional arrays efficiently.
    - branch/tag used: rel-0.8.2 tag
    - Justification: Stable and well tested
    - Source_Directories:
        - /home/ec2-user/src/Theano
- TensorFlow: TensorFlow™ is an open source software library for numerical computation using data flow graphs.
    - branch/tag used : r0.10 branch
    - Justification : Stable and well tested
    - Source_Directories :
        - /home/ec2-user/src/tensorflow
- Torch: Torch is a scientific computing framework with wide support for machine learning algorithms that puts GPUs first. It is easy to use and efficient, thanks to an easy and fast scripting language, LuaJIT, and an underlying C/CUDA implementation.

- branch/tag used : rel-0.8.2 branch
- Justification : No other stable branch or tag available
- Source_Directories :
    - /home/ec2-user/src/torch
- CNTK: CNTK - Microsoft Cognitive Toolkit - is a unified deep-learning toolkit by Microsoft Research.
    - branch/tag used : v2.0beta2.0
    - Justification : Stable release
    - Source_Directories :
        - /home/ec2-user/src/cntk

Python 2.7 and Python 3.5 Support

Python2.7 and Python3.5 are supported in the AMI for the following Deep Learning Frameworks:

1. Caffe
2. Tensorflow
3. Theano
4. MXNet

CPU Instance Type Support

The AMI supports CPU Instance Types for all frameworks. MXNet is built with support for Intel MKL2017 DNN library support. If you want to use the caffe binary for the CPU instance, then you should use the binary inside /home/ec2-user/src/caffe_cpu/

CNTK Python Support

You can run CNTK for Python inside a conda environment. To do this:

```
1 cd /home/ec2-user/src/anaconda3/bin
2    source activate cntk-py34
```

GPU Drivers Installed

- CuDNN 5.1
- NVIDIA 352.99
- CUDA 7.5

Launching Deep Learning Instance

Choose the flavor of the AMI from the list below in the region of your choice and follow the steps at:

EC2 Documentation to launch G2 Instance

Testing the Frameworks

The Deep Learning frameworks have been tested with MNIST data. The AMI contains scripts to train and test with MNIST for each of the frameworks. The test checks if the validation accuracy is above a specific threshold. The threshold is different for each of the frameworks.

The scripts are available in the /home/ec2-user/src/bin directory.

The following scripts test the various frameworks:

/home/ec2-user/src/bin/testAll : tests all frameworks

/home/ec2-user/src/bin/testMXNet : tests MXNet

/home/ec2-user/src/bin/testTheano : tests Theano

/home/ec2-user/src/bin/testTensorFlow : tests TensorFlow

/home/ec2-user/src/bin/testTorch : tests Torch

/home/ec2-user/src/bin/testCNTK : tests CNTK

The following tests have been run against each of the frameworks:

- MXNet: This example inside the MXNet repository. Validation accuracy threshold tested for is 97%.
- Tensorflow: This example inside the keras repository. Validation accuracy threshold tested for is 95%.
- Theano: The same example above. Validation accuracy threshold is 95%.
- Torch: This example inside the Torch tree. Validation accuracy threshold is 93%.
- Caffe: This example inside the Caffe repository. Validation accuracy threshold is 98%.
- CNTK: This example inside the CNTK repository. Validation accuracy threshold is 97%.

Amazon Linux AMI

Amazon Linux based Deep Learning AMIs are available in the following regions:

- eu-west-1(DUB)
- us-east-1(IAD)
- us-west-1(PDX)

References

MXNet

Caffe

Theano

TensorFlow

Torch

CNTK

Test Environments

- Built and Tested on g2.2xlarge.
- Also tested on g2.8xlarge, p2.16xlarge, c4.4xlarge.

AWS Deep Learning AMI Windows Release Archive

- Release Note Details for Deep Learning AMI (Windows 2016) Version 1.0
- Release Note Details for Deep Learning AMI (Windows 2012 R2) Version 1.0

Release Note Details for Deep Learning AMI (Windows 2016) Version 1.0

AWS Deep Learning AMI

The AWS Deep Learning AMI are prebuilt with CUDA 8 and 9, and several deep learning frameworks.

Highlights of the Release

1. CUDA 8 and 9
2. CuDNN 6 and 7
3. NCCL 2.0.5
4. CuBLAS 8 and 9
5. OpenCV 3.2.0
6. SciPy 0.19.1
7. Conda 5.01

Prebuilt Deep Learning Frameworks

- Apache MXNet: MXNet is a flexible, efficient, portable and scalable open source library for deep learning. It supports declarative and imperative programming models, across a wide variety of programming languages, making it powerful yet simple to code deep learning applications. MXNet is efficient, inherently supporting automatic parallel scheduling of portions of source code that can be parallelized over a distributed environment. MXNet is also portable, using memory optimizations that allow it to run on mobile phones to full servers.
    - branch/tag used: v0.12.0
    - Built with CUDA 8 and cuDNN 6.1
    - Justification: Stable and well tested
    - Source Directory:

        C:\MXNet
- Caffe: Caffe is a framework made with expression, speed, and modularity in mind.
    - branch/tag used: Windows branch, commit #5854
    - Built with CUDA 8 and cuDNN 5
    - Justification: Stable and well tested
    - Source Directory:

        C:\Caffe
- TensorFlow: TensorFlow™ is an open source software library for numerical computation using data flow graphs.
    - branch/tag used : v1.4
    - Built with CUDA 8 and cuDNN 6.1
    - Justification : Stable and well tested

- Source Directory:

  C:\ProgramData\Anaconda3\envs\tensorflow\Lib\site-packages

Python 2.7 and Python 3.5 Support

Python 2.7 and Python 3.6 are supported in the AMI for all of this installed Deep Learning Frameworks except Caffe2:

1. Apache MXNet
2. Caffe
3. Tensorflow

Instance Type Support

P3 instance type is not yet supported.

The AMI supports all other CPU Instance Types for all frameworks.

GPU Drivers Installed

- CuDNN 6 and 7
- Nvidia 385.54
- CUDA 8 and 9

Launching Deep Learning Instance

Choose the flavor of the AMI from the list below in the region of your choice and follow the steps at:

Launching a Windows Instance

Deep Learning AMI (Windows 2016) Regions

Windows 2016 AMIs are available in the following regions:

- US East (Ohio): ec2-us-east-2 - ami-6cc1ef09
- US East (N. Virginia): ec2-us-east-1 - ami-d50381af
- GovCloud: ec2-us-gov-west-1 - ami-d5018db4
- US West (N. California): ec2-us-west-1 - ami-0abf876a
- US West (Oregon): ec2-us-west-2 - ami-d3be62ab
- Asia Pacific (Mumbai): ec2-ap-south-1 - ami-6f1e5000
- Asia Pacific (Seoul): ec2-ap-northeast-2 - ami-9375d2fd
- Asia Pacific (Singapore): ec2-ap-southeast-1 - ami-5c64323f
- Asia Pacific (Sydney): ec2-ap-southeast-2 - ami-a0ca20c2
- Asia Pacific (Tokyo): ec2-ap-northeast-1 - ami-c6fe42a0
- Canada (Central): ec2-ca-central-1 - ami-4b82392f

- EU (Frankfurt): ec2-eu-central-1 - ami-9e7efcf1
- EU (Ireland): ec2-eu-west-1 - ami-8aee58f3
- EU (London): ec2-eu-west-2 - ami-09edf26d
- SA (Sao Paulo): ec2-sa-east-1 - ami-10bffa7c

References

- Apache MXNet
- Caffe
- TensorFlow

Test Environments

- Built on p2.16xlarge.
- Also tested on p2.xlarge, c4.4xlarge.

Release Note Details for Deep Learning AMI (Windows 2012 R2) Version 1.0

AWS Deep Learning AMI

The AWS Deep Learning AMI are prebuilt with CUDA 8 and 9, and several deep learning frameworks.

Highlights of the Release

1. CUDA 8 and 9
2. CuDNN 6 and 7
3. NCCL 2.0.5
4. CuBLAS 8 and 9
5. OpenCV 3.2.0
6. SciPy 0.19.1
7. Conda 5.01

Prebuilt Deep Learning Frameworks

- Apache MXNet: MXNet is a flexible, efficient, portable and scalable open source library for deep learning. It supports declarative and imperative programming models, across a wide variety of programming languages, making it powerful yet simple to code deep learning applications. MXNet is efficient, inherently supporting automatic parallel scheduling of portions of source code that can be parallelized over a distributed environment. MXNet is also portable, using memory optimizations that allow it to run on mobile phones to full servers.
  - branch/tag used: v0.12.0
  - Built with CUDA 8 and cuDNN 6.1
  - Justification: Stable and well tested
  - Source Directory:

    C:\MXNet
- Caffe: Caffe is a framework made with expression, speed, and modularity in mind.
  - branch/tag used: Windows branch, commit #5854
  - Built with CUDA 8 and cuDNN 5
  - Justification: Stable and well tested
  - Source Directory:

    C:\Caffe
- TensorFlow: TensorFlow™ is an open source software library for numerical computation using data flow graphs.
  - branch/tag used : v1.4
  - Built with CUDA 8 and cuDNN 6.1
  - Justification : Stable and well tested

- Source Directory:

  C:\ProgramData\Anaconda3\envs\tensorflow\Lib\site-packages

Python 2.7 and Python 3.5 Support

Python 2.7 and Python 3.6 are supported in the AMI for all of this installed Deep Learning Frameworks except Caffe2:

1. Apache MXNet
2. Caffe
3. Tensorflow

Instance Type Support

P3 instance type is not yet supported.

The AMI supports all other CPU Instance Types for all frameworks.

GPU Drivers Installed

- CuDNN 6 and 7
- Nvidia 385.54
- CUDA 8 and 9

Launching Deep Learning Instance

Choose the flavor of the AMI from the list below in the region of your choice and follow the steps at:
Launching a Windows Instance

Deep Learning AMI (Windows 2012 R2) Regions

Windows 2012 R2 AMIs are available in the following regions:

- US East (Ohio): ec2-us-east-2 - ami-93c0eef6
- US East (N. Virginia): ec2-us-east-1 - ami-3375f749
- GovCloud: ec2-us-gov-west-1 - ami-87018de6
- US West (N. California): ec2-us-west-1 - ami-04bf8764
- US West (Oregon): ec2-us-west-2 - ami-d2be62aa
- Asia Pacific (Mumbai): ec2-ap-south-1 - ami-221f514d
- Asia Pacific (Seoul): ec2-ap-northeast-2 - ami-1975d277
- Asia Pacific (Singapore): ec2-ap-southeast-1 - ami-5d67313e
- Asia Pacific (Sydney): ec2-ap-southeast-2 - ami-a2f71dc0
- Asia Pacific (Tokyo): ec2-ap-northeast-1 - ami-96fe42f0
- Canada (Central): ec2-ca-central-1 - ami-1a863d7e

- EU (Frankfurt): ec2-eu-central-1 - ami-cf78faa0

- EU (Ireland): ec2-eu-west-1 - ami-3eea5c47

- EU (London): ec2-eu-west-2 - ami-caeef1ae

- SA (Sao Paulo): ec2-sa-east-1 - ami-aabefbc6

References

- Apache MXNet
- Caffe
- TensorFlow

Test Environments

- Built on p2.16xlarge.
- Also tested on p2.xlarge, c4.4xlarge.

Document History for AWS Deep Learning AMI Developer Guide

The following table describes the documentation for this release of AWS Deep Learning AMI.

Change	Description	Date
New regions and new 10 minute tutorial	New regions added: US West (N. California), South America, Canada (Central), EU (London), and EU (Paris). Also, the first release of a 10-minute tutorial titled: "Getting Started with Deep Learning AMI".	April 26, 2018
Chainer tutorial	A tutorial for using Chainer in multi-GPU, single GPU, and CPU modes was added. CUDA integration was upgraded from CUDA 8 to CUDA 9 for several frameworks.	February 28, 2018
Linux AMIs v3.0, plus introduction of MXNet Model Server, TensorFlow Serving, and TensorBoard	Added tutorials for Conda AMIs with new model and visualization serving capabilities using MXNet Model Server v0.1.5, TensorFlow Serving v1.4.0, and TensorBoard v0.4.0. AMI and framework CUDA capabilities described in Conda and CUDA overviews. Latest release notes moved to https://aws.amazon.com/releasenotes/	January 25, 2018
Linux AMIs v2.0	Base, Source, and Conda AMIs updated with NCCL 2.1. Source and Conda AMIs updated with MXNet v1.0, PyTorch 0.3.0, and Keras 2.0.9.	December 11, 2017
Two Windows AMI options added	Windows 2012 R2 and 2016 AMIs released: added to AMI selection guide and added to release notes.	November 30, 2017
Initial documentation release	Detailed description of change with link to topic/section that was changed.	November 15, 2017

AWS Glossary

For the latest AWS terminology, see the AWS Glossary in the *AWS General Reference*.